Doug Wagner

# Boas

Everything About Selection, Care,
Nutrition, Diseases, Breeding, and Behavior

Filled with Full-color Photographs
Illustrations by David Wenzel

BARRON'S

# 2 C O N T E N T S

# CONSIDERATIONS BEFORE BUYING

*Fascinating in form and color, boa constrictors are the most popular large snake kept as pets today, but owning one comes with responsibilities. Smaller boa varieties offer a number of alternatives for prospective owners.*

## Why a Boa?

Ask people why they like boas and the answer is often their size. Although some small boa species may grow to only 2 feet (.6 m), the large boa constrictors remain the most popular by far. There's a natural, added appeal to a snake as big around as your arm when compared with their smaller cousins, no less so than the appeal of a Golden Retriever over a Chihuahua. The size of large boas also brings out their vibrant colors and bold patterns. Conversely, their size can also make them impractical for unprepared owners.

If you are considering the purchase of your first snake, buying a snake for a child under 13, or are unsure of your abilities or long-term commitment, a boa might not be the best choice. For that matter, a snake might not even be your best choice for a pet. Are you prepared to feed it cute little animals such as mice, rats,

*An orange red phase boa.*

or rabbits? There is no alternative. Can you accept getting bitten occasionally? I have enjoyed keeping snakes for more than 20 years, but it is not for everyone. Your first snake could get you hooked for life, or put you off snake keeping forever. If you are a beginner, I urge you to learn as much as you can before you buy, and to carefully evaluate your reasons for choosing a boa and your ability to keep it healthy. This book is intended to help you make an informed decision. If after reading it you are still not sure, then consider easing into your new hobby with a smaller and cheaper colubrid, such as a corn snake.

Typically calm when handled frequently, and hardy when a few specific care parameters are met, boas can make excellent pets. It must be remembered, however, that they are exotics, adapted to survive in their particular environment, not ours. This is not to say that you must recreate a portion of the Amazon rain forest in your home, but you will have to consider factors

*These boa constrictors are small and manageable now, but may grow to exceed 8 feet (2.5 m) within a few years.*

## Size

Not all boa species qualify as giants. Some, such as the rosy boas and sand boas, grow to just 2 to 3 feet (.6–.9 m), and only a few boa constrictor subspecies from South America are capable of exceeding 10 feet (3 m). Rarely will one exceed 12 feet (3.7 m) in captivity, with 8 to 10 feet (2–3 m) being more common. Somewhere in between are a number of midsize boas, including Dumeril's boas, rainbow boas, and tree boas (see species accounts, beginning on page 53).

Before purchasing one of the medium to large boa species, consider the full impact of its adult size. With proper feeding, that handsome little boa constrictor in the 10-gallon (38 L) aquarium will require a 20-gallon (76 L) aquarium by the end of its first year, and will rapidly progress through increasingly larger enclosures until a 5- or 6-foot (1.5–1.8 m) cage is needed. Large cages can be expensive, as well as heavy and cumbersome to move and clean. A big snake consumes big meals, and, if I may point out, defecates big messes! Depending on its thickness and absorbency, the entire cage substrate may be soaked and require replacement. Where will you put the snake while you clean its cage? A large boa is a powerful constrictor, capable of wrapping itself around furniture, fixtures, or people. Putting one back into its cage can often turn into a wrestling match, typically with the animal becoming more and more agitated. A very large specimen is capable of caus-

such as temperature and humidity. In addition to your obligations to your boa come obligations to yourself and to those around you, to be a responsible snake owner. If you fully understand these obligations and are prepared to meet the challenge, then a boa could be for you.

The poorest reason for obtaining a boa is to impress others. If you eagerly anticipate the attention and reaction to your new pet, I strongly urge you to reconsider. The appearance of any large constrictor in public, whether escaped, set free, or in the hands of an irresponsible owner, puts the entire herpetocultural community at risk. If you crave attention, buy a flashy red sports car instead.

ing death should it wrap around a person's neck and constrict, although deaths from boas are almost unheard of.

As with any pet, boas may occasionally bite the hand that feeds them. Even the most docile boa can be startled or mistake your hand for a tasty rodent. Multiple rows of sharp teeth are capable of inflicting a painful bite, especially from a large specimen. A typical defensive bite is quick, and over before you can react, but in a feeding response the snake may not release immediately. The natural reaction to pull away a hand may do additional damage to you or cause injury to the snake.

One last consideration regarding size: What are your future plans? Your boa may live 20 years or longer. Marriage, college, job transfers, and having children are just a few of the lifestyle changes that could affect your collection. If the time arrives when your snake must go, you may find the market for a sizable boa constrictor to be quite small, and your local zoo or animal pound will probably not be interested. But don't even consider releasing your boa in the woods; not only is it irresponsible and cruel—but in most places it's illegal.

## Temperament

The popularity of boas attests to their gentle disposition. With a reasonable amount of human interaction, most boas will retain their good-natured demeanor throughout life. Exceptions do exist, however, at the individual and the species level.

Imported, wild-caught adults are often irritable and take time to adjust to captivity. Such imports may also be finicky eaters, and commonly harbor internal and external parasites.

They are therefore best left to experienced keepers knowledgeable about detecting and treating these conditions.

Not all boa species contribute to the docile reputation of the group. Tree boas, rainbow boas, and even a few boa constrictor subspecies have somewhat questionable reputations. These should also be left to experienced keepers. Notes on temperament have been provided for each boa profiled in the section beginning on page 53.

## Where to Buy Your Boa

### Pet Shops

Finding boa constrictors has always been as easy as visiting your local pet shop. The vast majority of boas seen are common boa constrictors (*Boa constrictor imperator*), sometimes referred to as Colombian or Central American boas, which are imported in large numbers for the pet trade. Pet shops may carry a mix of captive-bred and imported snakes without knowing their source or history, so be especially diligent when examining any prospective purchase. Imported boas are often highly stressed, dehydrated, and heavily parasitized.

### Reptile Stores

Specialty pet stores devoted to reptiles typically offer a variety of imported and captive-bred animals, but are more likely to have detailed background information on the animals they sell. A reputable store will not hesitate to share the source of the boa you are interested in buying. They are also a good source for cages and other required items, as well as helpful advice.

# TIP

### Conservation

Protect wild populations by purchasing only captive-bred boas whenever possible and supporting ecosystem protection groups such as The Nature Conservancy.

### Breeders

For healthy boas, nothing beats buying directly from a reputable breeder. Reptile magazines carry ads for breeders, as well as listings for upcoming breeder shows. Herpetological societies are also a good place to find breeders and advice on where to obtain the best snakes.

### Mail Order

Although it may sound risky, don't discount buying snakes from distant sources and having them shipped to you. Many breeders maintain up-to-date web sites, some with pictures of each snake available for sale. Major shipping carriers offer same-day or overnight delivery to your door. By dealing with a reputable dealer with a fair guarantee, the rewards of mail-order snakes can far outweigh the risks.

### Cost

Many of the commonly kept and bred boas can be purchased for less than $100. Expect to pay more for rainbow boas, emerald tree boas, the Madagascar boas, and uncommon subspecies or exceptional colors and patterns. Designer boa morphs often run into many thousands of dollars.

# Regulations

Several levels of regulation may affect your ability to own a snake, or a particular species of snake. If you rent a house or apartment, check your lease to be sure that keeping snakes is not prohibited. Next, check the local ordinances of your city or town.

State wildlife agencies, besides protecting threatened or endangered native species, often set rules pertaining to animal housing and transportation. These rules may affect cage size and design, limit snake length, or restrict the number of animals kept or housed together. A permit to keep snakes may be required. Check the government section of your phone book for the number of the appropriate state wildlife agency.

National and international regulations, such as the Endangered Species Act and the Convention on International Trade in Endangered Species (CITES), restrict, prohibit, or require additional paperwork for the importation, transport, or keeping of endangered species. With their business at stake, however, it is

*For snakes that are unfamiliar or known to bite, use a firm but gentle grasp behind the head. Such restraint is also required for force-feeding, inspecting the mouth, or removing unshed eyecaps.*

*Large snakes must be properly supported when held but should not be placed around the neck. The snake is an unusually large Dumeril's boa.*

*Defensive posture of gaping mouth and hissing, sometimes bluff and sometimes not, is common to many boa constrictors, like this Argentine boa.*

unlikely that your pet shop or reptile store is offering illegal specimens.

## Choosing a Healthy Snake

If you have thought it through and concluded that a boa is right for you, then let's make sure you get a healthy one. Before you even touch it, examine your candidate and its enclosure. Is the cage filthy? Do any of its cagemates look sick? Look for partially open mouths, wheezing, and bubbles or discharge from the nostrils. These are symptoms that should send you to another cage, or to another source altogether. Respiratory diseases are often contagious, with the potential to wipe out an entire collection.

Look closely around the eyes and along the back. Tiny moving brown or black dots are

mites, bloodsucking parasites that spread quickly and can infest an entire reptile collection (see Mites, page 45). Fine, white specks may be mite droppings.

Now it is time to pick up your future pet. Check again for the above symptoms. Also check the mental groove, a narrow gap between the scales under the chin, as it is a favorite spot for mites. Your boa should be crawling slowly in your hands, its tongue flicking steadily. The body should be smooth and firm, free of sores, scars, or unusual lumps. The eyes should be bright, clear, and alert, and the mouth should close completely and naturally. Grasping the snake firmly but gently behind the head, carefully force the mouth open with the side of a pen or other smooth, thin object. The mouth should be clean and light pink or white, and free of open lesions, discoloration, or cheesy material that could indicate mouth rot.

Finally, ask the seller for any additional information about your boa, such as when and what your snake ate last, and if it has shed recently. Is it a male or female? Most reptile stores and breeders sell their offspring correctly sexed, or will make the determination on the spot. If you are unsure about anything, now is the time to ask.

# Your Responsibilities Begin

Now that you have joined the proud ranks of boa owners, it is time to get your snake home and set up. A cloth bag such as a pillowcase, tied at the top, is ideal for transporting your new pet. Do not place the bag on the dashboard, or run into the grocery store and leave it in a hot car. Excessive heat can cause death within minutes.

You should also have several items of standard equipment for housing and handling your boa.

✔ Secure cage, or tank with secure lid
✔ External heat source
✔ Lighting, if desired
✔ Water dishes large enough for your boa to soak in
✔ Hide boxes or other shelters
✔ Substrate; newspaper and aspen shavings are most common
✔ Climbing branches or secure perches
✔ Thermometer, with hygrometer for tropical species
✔ Work gloves and/or snake hook for safe handling
✔ Long forceps or tongs for offering food items

## Quarantine

Have a cage waiting when you arrive home, in a separate room from any other reptiles already owned. A one- to three-month quarantine period should be used to evaluate a new arrival and ensure that it is disease-free. If you already own other boas or pythons, a longer quarantine of up to one year will help protect them from the growing threat of IBD, or inclusion body disease, an untreatable and always fatal retrovirus. If new arrivals are added during the quarantine period, the process starts anew for all snakes in the same room. Even if you plan to house your boa in a large or elaborate cage, you should use a small temporary cage during the quarantine period, with only a hide box, a water dish big enough to soak in, and newspaper for substrate. If mites are found, you'll be glad you kept your new snake in simple quarters.

*Captive-bred boas, like this juvenile Guyana red-tail boa constrictor, are usually healthier than imported specimens.*

## Getting Acclimated

Your new boa has been stressed, so resist the urge to hold it or look in on it too often. Give it a few days to get acclimated to its new environment. A temperature of 83 to 86°F (28–30°C) is optimum at this time, aiding any unfinished digestion and boosting the immune system. Do not try to feed it for the first week. If you have other reptiles, always clean and handle quarantined animals last. Wash your hands when finished, and never transfer cage items or uneaten food from your quarantine area to your main collection. Watch for mites, either on the snake or drowned in the water dish, and, if found, begin treatment as suggested under the section of this book on external parasites (beginning on page 45).

## Record Keeping

Begin keeping records immediately of each feeding, defecation, shedding, and medical problems or treatments. Past records can be a valuable source in identifying and dealing with variations in a snake's normal behavior.

# The Perils of a Large Collection

Snakes, in their infinite variety, are like the proverbial Lays potato chip—it's hard to be satisfied with just one. If your first experience with a pet snake is a good one, and I sincerely hope it is, the chances are good that you'll get the urge to try your hand at breeding it, or to explore additional species as well. Just remember that these are not coins or stamps that can be collected with little more effort than an initial outlay of cash, but living, breathing animals that are fully dependent on us for their very lives. Unless

*Most boa constrictors found in pet shops are common boas (**Boa constrictor imperator**), usually from Colombia.*

you are willing and able to devote the same amount of time, attention, and care to each new arrival, your snakes will begin suffering from neglect. Cages may get cleaned less often or not as thoroughly. Handling becomes less frequent, resulting in a previously docile snake reverting to its instinctive, defensive ways. As collections increase, cage sizes decrease. The dangers of parasites and diseases are compounded and their treatment made more difficult. Less frequent close observation can mean that symptoms of distress or disease go unnoticed.

It may be a tough decision, but when daily care becomes an assembly-line chore rather than a relaxing pastime, it is time to reevaluate your priorities. Decide which species within your collection are the closest to your ideal, and consider selling the rest. Even if you can handle a large collection, keeping snakes with similar caging, feeding, and breeding requirements can simplify your hobby.

# UNDERSTANDING BOAS

*Understanding your snake's basic anatomy and needs will help explain how and why they do the things they do, and what you will need to provide to keep them healthy and comfortable.*

## Basic Anatomy

Over their long course of evolution, snakes have lost more than just legs. Ears and even the entire left lung have virtually disappeared in many species. Other paired organs, such as kidneys and ovaries or testes, have been moved around to get in line, instead of residing side by side. The taxonomic family Boidae, which includes the subfamilies *Boinae* (true boas), *Erycinae* (sand, rosy, and rubber boas), and *Pythoninae* (pythons), is a group of primitive, less-evolved snakes. Boids still retain a functional left lung and vestiges of the pelvic girdle. Small claws, or spurs, remnants of the hind legs, can often be found on either side of the snake's cloaca, particularly on males.

An incredibly flexible jaw, elastic skin, and long stomach allow snakes to take advantage of huge sizes and quantities of prey when available, and an efficient digestive system and slow metabolism ensure survival during long,

*Brazilian rainbow boa.*

lean periods. A sensitive tongue that tastes the air, and in some species sensory pits that detect the body heat of prey, all combine to make snakes the marvelous and intriguing creatures they are today.

## Mouth

A snake's mouth is uniquely adapted to the type and large size of the prey that must pass through it. The bones of the lower jaw are not

## TIP

### Snakebite

Boas are nonvenomous, but a bite can be startling. Almost every snake owner gets bitten sooner or later. Dedicated keepers consider "taking a bite" an unfortunate but acceptable part of the hobby they love.

affixed to the skull as ours are, nor connected at the chin. Muscles and ligaments allow each side to drop down and be pushed forward, alternatingly grabbing hold of prey and pulling it farther into the throat as the other side moves forward for a new grip. Once past the jaws, the prey is moved along to the stomach by muscle contractions and S-shaped curves of the body.

## Teeth

These are arranged in a single row on the bottom and two rows on top. They are relatively small compared with most mammals, but are needle sharp and curved inward for holding prey. The phrase *relatively small* loses its meaning as boas grow, and does not apply at all to

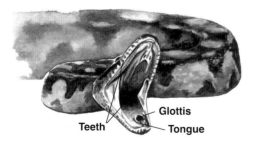

The inside of a snake's mouth. Note the glottis, or windpipe, at the bottom of the mouth, which allows breathing even while swallowing large prey.

*A snake's elastic skin, of which the scales are only a part, stretches to allow passage of large prey during swallowing.*

emerald tree boas, whose unusually large canine-like teeth earned them the Latin name *Corallus caninus*. A bite from a small boa often results in two mirror-image, horseshoe-shaped rows of tiny punctures from the teeth of the top and bottom jaws, with little pain but sometimes a great deal of blood. A bite from a very large boa, however, can be very painful. Wash any snakebite thoroughly with an antibacterial soap.

## Windpipe

At the bottom of a snake's mouth is the opening of the glottis, or windpipe. This amazing adaptation allows the snake to extrude the windpipe past large prey while swallowing. When disturbed, some boas may open the mouth and exhale loudly, producing a very loud hissing sound as the air exits the glottis. This is the only oral sound snakes make, as they have no vocal cords. The glottis does not branch off directly to the nasal passages as in humans. The external nasal openings are connected instead to openings in the snake's palate. In cases of respiratory disease or mouth rot, mucus may plug the internal nasal openings, forcing the snake to open its mouth to breathe.

## Tongue

The deeply forked tongue, a trademark of all snakes, is attached to the floor of the mouth in front of the windpipe. Thought by some to be a stinger of some sort, the tongue is actually quite harmless, and is the snake's primary means of identifying the objects around it. Tiny odor particles in the air are picked up by the soft, deli-

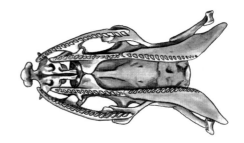

*Once seized, prey animals have difficulty escaping from the rows of sharp teeth, curved toward the throat.*

cate tongue as it flicks in and out through a small notch in the rostral (nose) scale. Once retracted, the tongue is inserted into a depression in the roof of the mouth, the Jacobson's organ, where the particles are "tasted" and identified. Food, mates, enemies, a familiar hiding place—all can be identified with a single flick of a snake's tongue.

# Sight and Sound

All boas have eyes with elliptical pupils, suited for efficient light gathering during nocturnal foraging. Their eyes are often colored to blend in with the color or pattern of the head. Snakes do not have moveable eyelids, and therefore do not blink. Instead, each eye is covered and protected by a clear ocular scale, also referred to as the eyecap, spectacle, or brille. The eyesight is moderately good for short distances, alerting the snake to movement in its vicinity and directing an accurate strike if necessary, but it is the tongue that determines just what the object is.

Snakes have no external ears and are almost completely deaf to airborne sounds. They do, however, retain remnants of the inner ear that are sensitive to vibrations traveling through the ground, and possibly very low frequency sound waves. Think of that before placing your stereo speakers on top of your snake cage and cranking up the heavy metal. I once placed the cage of an emerald tree boa on top of a small refrigerator during a space shortage in my snake room. It wasn't until my forehead touched the

glass one day that I realized the poor snake was housed in a permanent vibrator whenever the refrigerator was running!

# Locomotion

Snakes owe their unequaled flexibility to the fact that their backbone consists of hundreds of vertebrae. Each vertebra is attached to a pair of ribs, and each pair of ribs controls one ventral scale. A snake can literally walk itself forward in a straight line using its ribs. More often, snakes use a combination of rib walking and pushing coils of the body against the ground and other objects in their classic serpentine movement to get around. Snakes are awkward and uncomfortable when placed on very smooth surfaces such as glass.

Speed is rarely an issue of concern when dealing with boas. Unless agitated, boas take life at a slow, relaxed pace, another of their advantages over some of the more nervous colubrids.

# Defecation and Urination

Defecation and urination occur through the cloaca at the base of the tail. Water is conserved by passing urates in a semisolid form, typically appearing as a white pasty or sandy substance, either separately or in conjunction

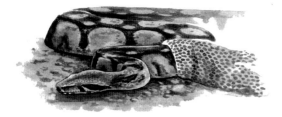

*Regular shedding of the epidermis permits growth and aids in eliminating external parasites. Young snakes shed more frequently than adults.*

with the passing of feces. In well-hydrated animals, a great deal of liquid may also be expelled, whereas dehydrated specimens may pass only solid, rock-hard balls of uric acid.

Feces contain waste products, including feathers and hair, the only part of prey animals that cannot be digested by the strong stomach acids. Boas do not defecate as often or as quickly after feeding as do colubrids, one of their advantages as pets. A boa fed weekly may defecate only once every one to three weeks. Well-formed stools are an indication of good health. Runny, foul-smelling stools, or those containing blood, mucus, or green bile, may be signs of disease or internal parasites. Consult your veterinarian if these appear.

# Thermoregulation

Like all reptiles, boas are ectothermic (cold-blooded) and have dry, scaly skin. The scales are actually tough folds of skin, not plates that can be scraped off, as on a fish. Most boas have smooth scales, although some have keeled scales or a combination of both. Not having to generate heat internally greatly reduces the body's demand for fuel, but requires that snakes spend much of their time using external elements for regulating body temperature to the optimum level for muscle activity, digestion, and disease resistance. While the sun provides heat from above, solar

collectors such as rocks, logs, roads, and even the ground itself accelerates the process from below, allowing the snake to reduce its exposure in the open. When things get too hot, snakes search out shade or water, or go underground where it is cooler. This need for self-thermoregulation is carried over into captivity. Whether heat is provided from above or below, it is a crucial component of successful care.

# Growth and Shedding

Growth in boas will depend largely upon the frequency and amount of feeding. As a rule, the first two years will produce rapid growth. Some breeders overfeed juveniles in an attempt to achieve breeding size more quickly, with mixed results. The outcome is more often obesity, small litter sizes, and a shortened lifespan.

All snakes need to shed their outer skin, or epidermis, as they grow. The first shed usually occurs several days after birth, and can be repeated as often as once a month for a rapidly

# TIP

## Shed Skins

Check shed skins closely for parasites, and to ensure that the skin from the eyecaps and tail is included. Moisten and gently remove any portion remaining on your boa.

*Snakes have no eyelids or external ears. The elliptical pupils common to all boas are clearly seen on this Hog Island boa.*

growing juvenile. An injured snake may also proceed through several sheds in rapid succession. Adults may shed only three or four times per year.

## The Shedding Process

The shedding process, or ecdysis, begins with the snake taking on a milky appearance, often most noticeable in the eyes, caused by secretions loosening the old epidermis. Colors and patterns darken and fade. Such snakes are referred to as being cloudy, opaque, or "in the blue." This condition typically lasts for a few days to a week, during which time the snake may not feed and may be irritable because of reduced vision. It is best not to handle or attempt to feed it. Provide a large water dish, however, as many snakes like to soak at this time. Remember to fill it only halfway, or you'll have an overflow when the snake curls up inside.

Two to three days before shedding, the snake's normal coloration returns. With certain exceptions, such as desert-dwelling rosy boas, low humidity can result in shedding difficulties. This is common in our artificially air-conditioned and heated indoor environments. If your snake regularly sheds in patches instead of in one piece, and will not soak in its water dish, try misting the snake and its enclosure with water once or twice daily to prepare for shedding. If you use any of

*Faded color and cloudy eyes indicate this Madagascar ground boa will shed its skin in about one week.*

the commercial plastic hide boxes, it is a good idea to mist the inside of the hide box as well.

Shedding begins with the snake rubbing its head against cage walls, rocks, branches, and even its own body to pull the outer skin loose from the edge of its mouth. The skin is then peeled back over the top of the head and under the chin, turning inside out as the snake literally crawls out of it. Often, the skin will continuously roll up as the snake crawls out, leaving a "doughnut" of shed skin when finished. If the

*A boa uses its tongue to identify and "taste" objects around it.*

After shedding, your snake's colors will be at their brightest. This is an especially good time for photography or, assuming it hasn't eaten during the shedding process, for feeding.

## Longevity

Boa constrictors are some of the longest-lived species of snakes, with records in excess of 20 years being common. A boa at the Philadelphia Zoological Gardens lived to the very old age of 40 years! Certainly, with proper care and good luck, your boa could live 10 to 15 years or longer.

## Interpreting Behavioral Clues

Snakes cannot talk. That is obvious. But they can tell you a lot by their actions. Even breeders with large collections come to recognize, and even expect, certain behaviors and preferences of individual animals. Perhaps the most obvious clue is temperature preference. If you have provided a temperature gradient in the cage, and your snake continuously remains at the warm end, it may not be warm enough. If the snake remains at the cool end, the cage is too hot.

snake is unable to get the skin off, you may have to mist it heavily, or soak it in a sink or bathtub, and work the skin off yourself, but never begin the process until the snake has started to shed on its own.

Shed skins should be checked to ensure that they include the eyecaps. One eyecap left on may not pose a problem; the snake may rub it off later, or it may come off with the next shedding. Continued failure of the eyecaps to come off, however, could lead to infection in or around the eyes. An unshed eyecap can be dealt with by moistening it with water, then removing it with blunt tweezers if there is a piece of attached skin to grab onto, or by rubbing a finger or damp towel backward across it while applying very gentle pressure.

A boa curled up in a water dish is not uncommon. But what if it stays in the dish for days, or has never before been seen soaking? Your records and the snake's appearance may indicate that it is shedding time. If a hide box has not been provided, your snake may be using the dish as a hiding place. Check the bottom of the dish closely for drowned mites. Heavy infestations of these tiny bloodsucking parasites

*Observe your boa's body language for signs of distress or contentment.*

can drive a snake into the water for relief. High temperatures and possibly even constipation may be other reasons for soaking.

A well-fed boa will often stay quietly curled in its hide box, with just the head poking out—an endearing habit compared with other snakes that stay completely hidden. When I don't see a head for two or three days, it's time to investigate, usually confirming my suspicion that the snake is preparing to shed. A snake cruising the cage tells me it is ready to eat, and one curled up uncharacteristically at the opposite end of the cage may be indicating that it left me a present under the hide box. Now, there's gratitude for you.

Lethargy, uncoordination, respiratory distress, or refusing to feed may require closer scrutiny. A boa that continually points its nose straight up may be suffering from a neurological disorder. Early detection and immediate quarantine of suspected problems could save your entire collection.

Boas are one of the few groups of snakes with an external feature that can often be used to accurately indicate sex. Male boas may possess spurs, clawlike remnants of their long-lost hind legs, on either side of the cloaca. In species where both males and females possess spurs, the male's are typically much larger, or, if the same size, more strongly recurved.

**Probing**

For species lacking spurs, or for juveniles with spurs that are just too small to be reliable, a sexing method referred to as *probing* is used. A narrow, blunt-tipped probe, lubricated with water or a nonspermicidal lubricating jelly, is inserted through the

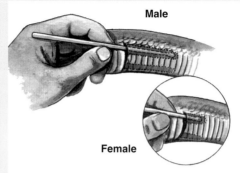

**Male**

**Female**

*Step 1—Gently insert the blunt probe into one of two small openings in the base of the tail, until resistance is felt. Mark the point of deepest penetration with your thumbnail before extracting the probe.*

*Step 2—Hold the probe against the tail, with your thumbnail again at the vent, to determine the depth probed in terms of subcaudal scales. Average probe depth will be 2 to 5 scales for females and 7 to 12 scales for males.*

snake's cloaca and into one of two openings into the base of the tail. In males, these openings are the inverted (inside-out) *hemipenes*. In females, these are musk glands, into which the probe should not penetrate as deeply as in the male. When resistance is felt,

a thumbnail is pressed against the probe at the spot where it enters the cloaca, thereby marking the depth of the probe. By then extracting the probe and holding it along the bottom of the tail, with the thumbnail again at the cloaca, the depth of the probe

*In species that have them, pronounced pelvic spurs are a good indication that the snake is a male. Spurs are typically shorter or absent in females.*

*Sexing probes. Probes are often sold in sets of various sizes, for probing very small to extremely large snakes. Seek professional guidance before attempting to probe snakes yourself.*

in relation to subcaudal scales (the scales on the bottom of the tail) can be determined. Although it varies by species, the average probe depth will be two to five scales for females and seven to twelve scales for males.

I strongly suggest that you let an experienced keeper guide you and demonstrate the probing technique first, and perhaps practice on a few less expensive snakes whose sex is already known. *Inserting a probe too far can cause injury or lead to infection.* The musk gland into which the probe is inserted in females is delicate and can accidentally be perforated, leading to the animal being incorrectly sexed as a male.

## "Popping"

Another method of sexing that works well with juveniles is "popping" the hemipenes. Again, let an experienced keeper demonstrate the technique to avoid injury to your snake. By holding the snake upside down, a thumbnail is pressed against the bottom of the tail below the cloaca, and then pushed upward toward the cloaca. The other thumb, pressed against the belly just above the cloaca, bends the snake slightly backward and pulls the vent open. If done correctly, in a male, one or both hemipenes will evert, or turn right side out, from the inside of the tail. This method can

*"Popping," or manually everting the hemipenes, can be useful in sexing juveniles. This method should also be demonstrated by a professional before you attempt it yourself.*

prove a male beyond a shadow of a doubt, but a "female" might just be a male that will not evert. Many breeders master this technique well enough to trust their judgment, but if in doubt, confirm a female by probing. Raising a pair of boas for years in preparation for breeding, only to find they're both males, could be frustrating.

Although most snakes purchased from professional breeders and reputable reptile pet shops will be accurately sexed, mistakes have been known to happen. If you are purchasing juveniles for future breeding projects, consider probing your animals again once you become comfortable with the procedure, especially if the size of the spurs do not support the original determination of sex.

# CAGING

*Form or function? Aesthetically pleasing enclosures made of natural materials can greatly increase the enjoyment of keeping a boa, but may also increase the work. Regardless of which approach you choose, commercial manufacturers today produce attractive, secure caging options in a variety of sizes.*

## Selecting a Cage

The only perfect cage is the one that satisfies all your needs and those of your boa. Typically, your final choice will be a compromise, but a number of factors must be considered:
- What type of boa?
- How big will it grow?
- How much do you want to spend?
- How much room do you have available?
- How many cages will you need?
- Does it need to be appealing to the eye, or just functional?

For a single snake or a very small collection, large attractive cages will do much to enhance your enjoyment of the hobby. Give your snake as much room as you can afford to, physically and financially. Constantly upgrading cage space can get expensive. Looking to the future

*Your boa's cage should measure about two-thirds the length of the snake.*

and your boa's adult size will save you money later on.

A good rule of thumb for cage space is to select a cage that is two-thirds the length of the snake. A 2-foot (.6 m) cage is adequate for rosy and sand boas, 3 to 4 feet (.9–1.2 m) for rainbow boas, and 4 to 6 feet (1.2–1.8 m) for most boa constrictors. Most boas are great climbers, and heavy branches allow them to make good use of vertical space. Arboreal species such as tree boas will require tall enclosures with a number of branches or perches. Cage height for nonarboreal species in a large or growing collection may have to be sacrificed to allow for stackable or shelved units.

### Specialty Cages

A number of companies produce affordable cages and multi-cage units specifically designed for reptiles, made out of easily cleaned materials such as glass, plastic, and melamine (lami-

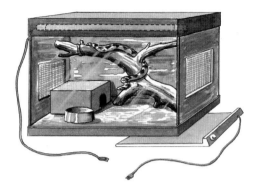

**Escapes**

Snakes are masters of escape. They will explore every crevice and exert amazing pressure on any door, lid, or screen that shows any hint of give.

*Basic cage setup for small to medium boas, with hide box, water dish, climbing branch, light fixture, and heating pad underneath. The hide box and water dish should always be at the cool end of the cage.*

nated fiberboard). Available options include door type, vent size and location, removable perches, cage-to-cage connectors, and prewired lighting or heating elements. Manufacturers of lightweight vacuum-formed plastic cages offer seamless enclosures with rounded corners and edges, eliminating crevices where liquid, bacteria, and mites can cause problems.

It is always best to house snakes individually, except during breeding. This reduces stress on the animals and the spread of parasites and diseases, and allows you to better monitor defecation, shedding, and other events. If you do house boas together, cage size should be increased and you must separate them for feeding. Once a snake detects the scent of food, its instinct is to strike whatever moves and then swallow it, even if it is a cage mate.

## Glass Aquarium

The most common cage used by beginners is the glass aquarium with a screen top. The small, ground-dwelling rosy and sand boas could live their entire lives in a 10-gallon (38 L) aquarium. If you have the space, I have always preferred the 20-gallon (76 L) size, especially if a lamp or other heating device is to be used at one end. Screen tops allow for excellent ventilation for dry-habitat species, although stacking is impossible and lights must be removed to open the lid. Another major drawback of screen tops is the absence or ineffectiveness of latching mechanisms. If a snug and secure top can be found, all boas can start off in such an aquarium, but few can stay in one for very long.

*Multi-cage unit for medium-sized boas. Professionally built and well-lighted cages make a handsome addition to any room.*

## Building Your Own Cage

If you like to build things, you might want to build your own cage. The interior will need to be water resistant and impervious to spills and high humidity. Silicon aquarium sealant should be used to seal all joints. Exposed, untreated wood should be avoided for the interior of cages, as it will absorb water and feces. When soiled, untreated wood is nearly impossible to clean and disinfect completely, resulting in bacterial growth. Uncovered Peg-Board or fiberboard may be weakened when wet, to the point of allowing a snake to push right through. If you intend to use newspaper as substrate, considering the size of your local paper when drawing up plans can save folding, cutting, or wasting paper later.

## Doors

Front-opening cages allow you to keep several cages in a vertical space, usually not actually stacked but shelved in a way that allows for lights to be placed on top. If high humidity is important, select or build a cage with small vent openings on the back or sides, and only minimal screening on top for lighting. Doors can be one of several types. A single sliding door of glass or Lexan offers great visibility, but requires clearance on either side to open the door, and cannot be fully opened. Bypass doors allow access to only half the cage at a time, a problem when a big boa decides it doesn't want to come out or go back inside. Hinged doors typically have a frame that reduces the view, but allows the cage to be opened fully.

*Rack system suitable for housing large numbers of juveniles, or small boas such as rosy and sand boas. Additional heat can be provided by using heating cable.*

## Latches

Regardless of the type of doors, secure latches or pins are required to keep your snake inside. Don't trust a tight fit or the weight of sliding glass to prevent escapes. Boas are strong and heavy, and they will get out. A thin rubber wedge firmly inserted between the overlap of sliding glass doors will help prevent them from being pushed open by your snakes. Where both snakes and children are present, a locking mechanism will protect each from the other.

# Rack Systems

For large numbers of adult rosy or sand boas, or juveniles of almost any species, nothing beats the simplicity of a rack system. A rack is nothing more than a set of shelves, typically constructed of moisture-resistant melamine or laminated wood, with each shelf holding one or more plastic storage boxes. By having the shelves built to the exact height and slightly deeper than the depth of the boxes to be used,

*This rack at Glades Herp, a reptile store, has clear boxes with lids in place, offering excellent visibility and security for snakes and customers.*

each shelf acts as the lid to the boxes below. A backing is required to prevent boxes from being pushed in too far. Peg-Board makes a good backing and increases ventilation. Shelves must be built to exact tolerances—too loose and snakes may escape or strangle, too tight and the boxes stick.

## Types of Boxes

Various suitable boxes are available, some rigid and clear, others flexible and opaque. Flexible Rubbermaid and Sterilite brand storage boxes in several sizes (shoe, sweater, blanket, etc.) can be found at discount and department stores (watch for sales after Christmas). I prefer the less-expensive Sterilite boxes in 15- and 32-quart (14–30 L) sizes. Because these boxes are the same height, racks are built wide enough to hold three 15-quart (14 L) and deep enough for two 32-quart (30 L) boxes per shelf.

Rack units should not be built much wider than this, as the units are extremely heavy and shelves will sag in the middle. Wheels are highly recommended for ease of movement.

## Ventilation

Ventilation is provided by drilling or burning a large quantity of airholes into all four sides of each box. Don't skimp on holes, particularly when housing low-humidity species. Burning holes with a soldering iron is quicker, makes smoother holes, and nearly eliminates the cracking and shattering that can occur from drilling. Heating for the unit can be provided by running heat tape or routering a groove for a heating cable across each shelf, 3 to 4 inches (8–10 cm) from the back. By cutting an opening at each end of the shelf, the heating element can be snaked (no pun intended) from shelf to shelf, and even from rack to rack, all connected to a timer and/or thermostat for temperature control. Side or back lighting is possible, but most rack users rely solely on ambient light from the front.

## Maintenance

Maintenance using this type of system is quick and easy: Slide a box out partway, replace the water dish and newspaper or other substrate, and slide the box back in. My rule is that if feces touch the plastic, the box must either be washed and disinfected or replaced. So long as care is exercised in pushing boxes in, racks are virtually escape-proof. The lack of screen prevents active or nervous snakes from rubbing the nose raw. Check the underside

*Arboreal snakes, like this Amazon tree boa, do best in tall cages with numerous branches.*

of shelves from time to time during cleaning, as mold or mildew can result from inadequate ventilation.

# Substrate

Though not the most attractive or natural material, newspaper is by far the best substrate for large boas. Newspaper is inexpensive and plentiful (I have my substrate delivered to my driveway every day), and unlike other materials such as gravel or wood chips, it can easily be completely discarded and replaced after every defecation or water spill, no matter how small. Failure to adequately clean and disinfect cages is one of the primary causes of health problems in snakes.

Some keepers maintain small boas on sand, gravel, or wood shavings. One possible drawback is the occasional ingestion of such substrate during feeding. In small amounts, this usually poses no problem, but impaction and blockage of the digestive tract is possible. As with any substrate, complete removal of soiled areas or water spills is required to prevent bacteria or mold buildup.

**Caution:** Cedar and pine should never be used in snake enclosures, either as a substrate or in hiding places, because of their irritating fumes.

# Temperature

Proper temperature is critical for maintaining good health in all reptiles. With a few exceptions, boas are tropical species adapted to very warm temperatures. Without sufficient heat,

adequate digestion and disease resistance cannot be maintained.

Providing a temperature gradient or a warm basking area in your cage through the use of a heat lamp, heat tape, or heating pad at one end will allow your boa to choose the best temperature for its needs. Under-cage heaters should warm only one-third to one-half of the enclosure. The warm end or basking area should be at the high end of the snake's preferred range, around 85–92°F (29–33°C) for most tropical boas, with the remainder of the cage in the low 80s°F (27–29°C). A drop of several degrees at night is recommended, but except during brumation in preparation for breeding, and especially after feeding, prolonged exposure to temperatures below 80°F (27°C) must be avoided.

Regardless of the heating element used, care must be exercised to avoid overheating the cage, burning the snake, or burning your house down. Always follow manufacturer instructions for safe use. Before returning any snakes to the cage, check temperatures carefully after the heat has been on for one to two hours. A rheo-

*Some snakes, like this Amazon Tree boa, require habitats with high humidity.*

stat or thermostat may be required to more accurately adjust the heat to the desired level. An incandescent lightbulb can get extremely hot, and must be placed outside the cage and separated by screening so that the snake cannot touch it. Make sure the fixture is secure, well ventilated, and away from combustible materials such as paper or curtains.

Optimally, the snake will spend most of its time somewhere in the middle of the cage, indicating that a preferred midrange temperature has been selected. If your snake spends all of its time at one end, the cage may be too warm or too cool.

# Lighting and Photoperiod

Although it is currently accepted that snakes do not require full-spectrum lights like other reptiles, many keepers still use them, both for their color quality and for the more natural ultraviolet light produced.

Regardless of the source, snakes should be provided with a daily cycle, or photoperiod, of light and darkness. Lights should never be left on 24 hours a day. If enough ambient light is present from windows or skylights, no additional light is needed.

Additional cage lighting can be in the form of incandescent or fluorescent bulbs, connected to a timer to regulate photoperiod. Photoperiod can be a constant 12 hours on and 12 off, or it can be changed occasionally to match the natural seasonal fluctuations of day and night. Before and during winter brumation in preparation for breeding, many breeders will reduce daylight hours, imitating the shorter days of winter as part of their seasonal breeding cues.

# Humidity

The most common humidity-related problem seen in snakes is dry skin and poor shedding. Even in regions where high humidity is the norm outdoors, air-conditioning and heating can dry out the environment indoors. Drafty conditions accelerate the drying process. This problem can usually be avoided by providing a water dish or pool large enough for the snake to soak in. A large dish or pool also serves to increase cage humidity through evaporation. If the snake continues to have problems, or spends too much time soaking, reduce the amount of ventilation to further increase the humidity. A daily misting of the snake and its enclosure may be required. Do not soak the cage and substrate, or overly restrict ventilation, as mold and fungus may result. Room humidifiers are also an option, if all species in the room need higher humidity. A very helpful tip is to use distilled or spring water in humidifiers and misting bottles, as calcium and lime deposits in tap water will quickly encrust humidifier heating elements and cage glass.

Rainbow boas and tree boas are known to require high humidity. I use large water dishes and smaller ventilation openings for my rainbow boas, and mist them only just before shedding, although one juvenile did require daily mistings during his first year. Because of the increased risk of mold and fungus from damp cages, I suggest letting each snake's actions, skin appearance, and shedding results determine whether daily misting is needed.

# TIP

## The Pinch Test
When pinched and released, your boa's skin should snap back into place. If the fold remains, take immediate action to increase water intake and raise cage humidity.

For sand boas and rosy boas, high humidity is not only unnecessary, but detrimental. For these species, small water dishes and excellent ventilation are a must. Some keepers offer water to these boas only once or twice a week, removing the water dish after the snake has had an opportunity to drink. I prefer good ventilation and leaving the water dish in the cage.

Most electronics and hardware stores carry a variety of combination digital thermometers and hygrometers for simultaneous monitoring of temperature and humidity.

# Cleaning and Disinfecting

Assuming you have acquired parasite- and disease-free snakes, failure to maintain a clean enclosure is perhaps the number one cause of serious problems in captive snakes. The inability to distance itself from feces means the snake is exposed to higher concentrations of bacteria than would be encountered in the wild. In high enough concentrations, or when combined with a weakened immune system resulting from disease

*While the eyes of this boa look bright and healthy, swelling and cloudy color eyes can be symptoms of eye infections.*

## TIP

### Perches
For easier cleaning, use perches or benches securely attached to cage walls instead of resting on the floor. The snake is often up out of the way and does not need to be moved while the floor substrate is replaced.

or suboptimum cage temperatures, such bacteria can quickly overwhelm the snake's natural defenses. Simply replacing wet or soiled substrate is not enough. A snake crawling through excrement will spread it wherever he crawls—through the water dish, over the hide box, up the glass. What you can't see can still hurt your snake.

The best way to clean a cage thoroughly is to remove the snake and discard any disposable substrate or hide box. The enclosure and all reusable objects such as the water dish, plastic hide box, or perches should be washed and disinfected with a bleach or other disinfectant solution, and allowed to air-dry. Some cleaning solutions such as Roccal-D are also virucidal, giving an added protection against disease, but they can be very expensive. A solution of warm, soapy water (liquid dish soap) and 10 percent bleach makes an effective yet inexpensive disinfectant. Allow items to soak 15 to 20 minutes for best results.

If you wish to clean only a portion of the cage, do not spray cleaning fluids inside with the snake or water dish present. Instead, spray them onto a paper towel or rag well away from the cage and then wipe the inside of the enclosure. Good ventilation is a must.

# Making Your Boa Feel at Home

Many herpetoculturists are turning to natural vivaria these days to enhance the life of their pets, and perhaps to achieve the true purpose of keeping these pets in our homes—to bring nature into our unnatural human habitats. Unfortunately, most boas are just too large for such lushly planted vivaria. The focus for boa enclosures should be on simplicity, functionality, and ease of maintenance.

*Provide a water dish large enough for drinking and for soaking.*

## The Hide Box

A hide box is an important cage component and should generally be placed at the darker or cooler end of the enclosure. Large boa constrictors seem content to remain in the open more than juveniles, perhaps because in the wild they have few enemies at this size and just as few places large enough to hide in. But even boas that ordinarily spend little time in the hide box may use it while opaque, after eating, or if stressed. Types of suitable hiding places are limited only by your imagination. Any object that provides a dark, snug fit will suffice. If one is not provided, snakes will typically hide under the substrate. The entrance to the box should be large enough for the snake to crawl through after a big meal. For small boas, any empty household cardboard box can be used, including shoe, cereal, or bathroom tissue boxes. Avoid boxes with strong odors, or ones that formerly contained substances that could be harmful to your snake, such as laundry detergent. Durable commercially produced plastic hide boxes are available in various sizes and colors, and can be washed and reused as needed. Faux stone caves, though strong and attractive, can be difficult to clean thoroughly when defecated on. For very large boas, inverted rubber or plastic tubs with an entrance hole cut out make good, strong hiding places.

## Branches or Perches

A strong branch or perch will allow your boa to exercise its climbing instincts while using the vertical space of the cage. Besides, it's fun to watch snakes climb. For very large boa constrictors in equally large enclosures, many keepers provide a bench or ledge for their snakes to lie on, sometimes even attaching heating pads to the underside, providing heat above and below the bench. Be sure that when heavy branches, benches, or rocks are used, it is impossible for them to collapse or fall onto your snake.

## Water Dishes

A water dish large enough to soak in is a necessity. The water dish should be replaced and washed twice a week, or whenever any foreign matter is observed in it; it is not unusual for snakes to defecate in the water dish.

# FEEDING

*Snakes require feeding only once every one to two weeks. Buying frozen rodents in bulk makes feeding more economical, healthful, and convenient than ever before.*

## What They Eat and How Often

All snakes are strictly carnivorous. For most boas, the preferred foods are rodents, other small mammals, and birds. Juveniles and some small species of boas may consume lizards or frogs, either occasionally or exclusively (refer to the species accounts beginning on page 53 for food preferences). Such a whole-animal diet provides all the vitamins and minerals required for growth and good health. Additional vitamin supplements are not needed, even for growing juveniles.

Opportunistic feeders in the wild, snakes are capable of swallowing extremely large sizes and quantities of prey when the chance presents itself, and of going long periods without food during lean times. As pets, it is better for them

*Madagascar tree boa.*

to be fed moderate amounts on a regular basis. Active or growing boas should be fed about once a week. One food animal of appropriate size to put a small bulge in the snake's stomach will suffice, or feed two if faster growth is desired. Large boa constrictors feeding on jumbo rats or rabbits, and less active species such as emerald tree boas, should be fed once every two to four weeks. Two smaller food animals are preferable to one larger one. Because prey items are swallowed whole, digestion is a slow process. Especially under suboptimum temperatures, a prey item that is too large may actually turn rancid inside the stomach and be regurgitated.

Chicken and other fowl are readily accepted by many boas; however, a diet of chicken often results in soft, foul-smelling stools. Uncooked chicken can also be a source of *Salmonella* bacteria. Most keepers will feed chicken only as a last resort for difficult feeders, or on newly imported specimens.

Your snake will tell you when it is hungry by exploring its cage. Don't be too quick to accommodate it, though. Snakes in the wild must search days and even weeks for a meal. The exercise will do your boa good, preventing problems such as obesity or constipation.

# Constricting

Mention the word *constrictor* to most non-herpetoculturists and the image that pops into mind is of huge boa constrictors crushing people and prey to death. All species of boas are constrictors, as are most other snakes that must subdue dangerous prey.

Despite the fact that boas are indeed very powerful constrictors, the "bone-crushing" reputation is undeserved. Not only do they not break any bones, but even a fairly large specimen can exert little more than a hearty hug around the abdomen of an average adult human. Care must be exercised, however, not to place boas longer than 6 feet (1.8 m) around the neck or leave them unsupervised with small children. Having an extra person around when handling snakes longer than 8 feet (2.5 m) is recommended. Constricting behavior while being handled is usually caused by the snake's fear of falling. If your boa becomes frightened and begins to constrict, remain calm and, beginning at the head or tail, unwrap it like a scarf.

To constrict its prey, a snake first grabs the animal with its sharp teeth, then quickly wraps one or more coils around it. The powerful coils are tightened whenever the prey exhales or relaxes its muscles, making it impossible for the prey to breathe. Death results fairly quickly from asphyxiation and the pressure exerted on the heart and circulatory system. When the

═══ TIP ═══

**Feeding Time**
Because most boas are nocturnal, feeding them in the evening often gets the best results.

prey has been dispatched, the snake relaxes its coils and begins swallowing. If the prey was not originally grabbed by the head, the snake may release it and search for the head, or simply walk its jaws along the prey until the nose is found. Prey swallowed headfirst will obviously go down much more easily than if swallowed backward, but don't be surprised or concerned if your boa occasionally forgets this. I once watched an Argentine boa constrictor consume a large rat sideways, folding it into a U-shape that seemed impossibly too wide to swallow. The truth is, there is very little those elastic jaws can't handle, and little that you can do to change things once swallowing has begun. If you can't bear to watch, don't.

After eating, it is perfectly normal for a snake to "yawn" as it moves its jaws back into place. Rubbing its mouth on the cage or cage accessories is also common.

# Live, Fresh–Killed, or Frozen?

Frozen rodents have a number of advantages over live prey. Live mice and rats have been known to severely injure and kill snakes—even large boas and pythons if they refuse to eat the prey—and must never be allowed to remain in the cage unobserved. Even in a powerful con-

*All boas are constrictors.*

strictor's coils, a feisty prey animal can take out the snake's eye with one quick bite. Why take the chance, when most snakes readily accept frozen-thawed rodents? Frozen rodents are also convenient and less expensive than live ones purchased in a pet shop, and freezing can reduce or eliminate parasites in food animals. A freezer full of appropriate-sized rodents ensures that when you're ready to feed them, each snake will get the correct type and size of food needed. Just be careful about letting your houseguests go snooping through your freezer!

If you do not have a reptile store or exotic pet shop nearby that offers frozen rodents, suppliers can be found in the classified ads of reptile magazines. Pricing is often based on the quantity ordered, so order up to a six-month supply or combine orders with other snake-keeping friends. Include expected off-feed periods such as shedding or brumation when calculating future needs. Frozen rodents are typically shipped by overnight carrier, packed in insulating Styrofoam. If it is available, request that dry ice be included, especially if your order is all small rodents or if the amount you ordered does not completely fill the shipping container.

Young mice and rats, referred to as *pinkies, fuzzies,* or *crawlers,* which have not yet developed sharp teeth, can safely be offered alive to smaller boas and even left in the cage overnight. For boas that need a larger meal, a safe alternative is to use stunned or freshly killed rodents instead. The most common stunning method is to grasp the rodent by the tail, swing it in an arc, and strike the back of its head sharply against a board or other hard object. A stunned rodent can recover, so keep your eye on it. Ideally, dispatching rodents yourself will be only a temporary requirement.

Some snakes simply will not eat rodents that have been frozen, but with a bit of patience, you can probably get your snake converted.

If your boa is in good health, offer only frozen-thawed food for several weeks. Try

*Madagascar ground boa dispatching prey by constriction.*

*Emerald tree boas ambush and swallow prey while hanging from a branch.*

## Offering Food

It is always amazing to me how quickly a snake that never bites defensively can determine that an approaching object is food. One flick of the tongue is usually all it takes, with a lightning-fast strike following in just a fraction of a second. A feeding strike can be more dangerous to a keeper than a defensive strike, because the snake intends to hold on. If you've been handling rodents, or if you have some alive or thawing in the same room, don't stick your hand in a cage. Even from across the room, your snake's sensitive tongue will be able to detect the odor. Of course, you don't want to feed your snake in a dirty cage, so complete your daily cage inspection and cleaning before bringing rodents into the same room.

### Using Live Prey

If you plan to feed live mice or rats purchased at a pet shop, the first thing to remember is that they like to start chewing through the bag or "critter carrier" cardboard box the

rodents of different types, sizes, and colors, offered both during the day and at night. If a defensive snake can be antagonized into striking at a frozen rodent, it may decide to hold on and eat it. A slightly warm rodent placed in the cage after dark and left overnight often gets good results.

Don't give up. With each feeding, try frozen prey first. Your boa may just surprise you and switch one day. Once a snake begins eating frozen prey, don't go back to live unless absolutely necessary.

moment they're put into it. They're also speedy runners and gifted high-jumpers—if any escape, you'll have a merry chase on your hands. One mouse in my bedroom eluded capture for three days, despite being spotted and even cornered several times! So, if you have a long drive home from the pet shop, take along a deep bucket. If not, have one ready when you get home into which you can dump the rodents. This also makes it easier to select the right size if you've bought several, and easier to grab hold of their tails. Make sure the snake is away from the cage door, and toss the rodent inside. Always keep an eye on the situation until you're sure the snake has dispatched his prey.

### Frozen-thawed

Frozen rodents must be fully thawed before use. I prefer to thaw them overnight in the refrigerator, then warm them slightly on a heating pad. Do not microwave or overheat rodents, as they may explode or break open during feeding—very unpleasant!

For feeding frozen-thawed food, a long set of forceps is an indispensable tool. Offering

*Four common mouse sizes for feeding snakes: pinky, fuzzy, hopper, and adult.*

food by hand is just an invitation to getting bitten. Some snakes will take the food from the forceps, whereas others merely like it dropped where they can take it at their leisure.

## Convincing a Difficult Feeder

Nothing in herpetoculture is quite so frustrating as a snake that acts hungry, but refuses to eat. I've actually watched snakes push frozen-thawed rodents around with their nose, as if thinking, "I smell it—maybe it's under this thing." It's enough to make a grown herpetoculturist cry, but in this hobby, patience is indeed a virtue. There are some short-term

*Force-feeding may be required as a last resort for snakes that refuse to eat. Gently force the dead prey item partially into the throat, and release slowly. Be patient and prepared to try again.*

circumstances under which your snake may stop feeding, and all you need to do is wait them out:

• Snakes often will not eat during their opaque period before shedding their skin.
• During breeding season, males may be more interested in mating than eating, even males you may consider too young to breed.
• Your snake may sense that it is winter, even if you have made the effort to keep the cage within a consistent temperature range.

If your snake is healthy, these short fasts should not be a cause for alarm. There are other possibilities, however, that will require action on your part.

• Examine the snake closely for indications of health problems or parasites. Consult with a qualified reptile veterinarian if you suspect something may be wrong.
• Is the cage warm enough? Cool temperatures can keep a snake from eating, and can cause health problems if it does eat.
• Is the snake stressed? Cagemates, excessive handling, and lack of hiding places could affect feeding.

If the snake appears healthy and the cage conditions are adequate, offer frozen-thawed food of different types and sizes, progressing to stunned, freshly killed, or live prey as required.

## Force-feeding

Force-feeding should be a last resort. With the snake resting on the floor of its cage or other level surface, grasp it firmly behind the head. With the other hand, force the nose of the food item into the snake's mouth and partially into the throat. Very slowly, release your hold on the snake, and try not to move. It may take a number of tries, but ideally the snake will finally decide to swallow the food.

Neonates can be force-fed parts of food animals, such as mouse tails or skinned chick legs; however, because of their small size, neonates could be injured during the strong restraint required for force-feeding. An alternative is to use a device called a pinky pump. Frozen-thawed pinkies and a small quantity of water (instead of water, one breeder I consulted uses a commercially offered reptile appetite stimulant called Stimulap) are placed into the syringe-like pinky pump, which purees the mice as they are injected through a small tube inserted down the snake's throat. The tube should be lubricated with vegetable oil or water before being inserted into the throat. Whenever possible, let an experienced person demonstrate proper force-feeding techniques before attempting them yourself.

# Regurgitation

Regurgitation in any snake should be taken very seriously, as it could be the first indication of a disease that may threaten your entire col-

*Desert snakes, such as this Rosy boa, need a dry climate.*

lection. It may also point to shortcomings in your husbandry techniques. Stress factors such as cagemates, the lack of a hiding place, or being handled too soon after feeding may also play a part. Unless a cause is obvious, immediate quarantine is suggested.

In my experience, most regurgitation results from meals that are too large or too frequent, and temperatures outside the optimum range. Because snakes swallow prey whole, digestion takes days, turning the process into a race between digestion and decay. Large prey items and cool temperatures slow digestion, whereas hot temperatures can accelerate decay. Food that remains in the stomach too long can release toxins that can harm or even kill a snake.

When feeding frozen-thawed, be sure to avoid rodents that have freezer burn or discolorations, have obvious deformities or tumors, or were previously thawed and refrozen. Be sure that frozen rodents are always completely thawed before use.

Sand or wood chips used as a cage substrate may adhere to food and be swallowed, occasionally becoming lodged in the digestive tract and causing a blockage. The water dish is another area that requires investigation. Replace the water dish twice each week, and whenever any foreign matter is seen or after the snake has been observed soaking.

The drug Flagyl, given orally at a dose of 50 milligrams per kilogram of body weight for three to five days, is a common medical treatment after regurgitation. Some keepers use compounds called probiotics, or direct-fed-microbials (DFMs). These products, such as NutriBAC, contain several types of intestinal flora beneficial for digestion, much like active cultures in yogurt.

After regurgitation, allow a few days under optimum temperatures and conditions, and then feed a single small food item. If regurgitation continues, take the snake and regurgitated rodent to your veterinarian for a culture.

Although the number of rodent suppliers is growing quickly, sometimes offering frozen rodents at prices 50 to 90 percent cheaper than live ones purchased at a pet shop, there are reasons that you may wish to breed your own. Snake breeders concerned about the quality and health of food items, or having large numbers of offspring to feed, may find it advantageous to maintain their own rodent breeding colony. So, too, will owners whose animals will accept only live prey. Having a rodent colony might appear at first to offer "free" food, but breeding rodents is not without its own expenses and drawbacks.

### Drawbacks

Before we get into the specifics of constructing a

*A good ratio for a small breeding colony is one male to three or four females. The male is on the right; the female is on the left.*

*Two possible cage setups for raising rodents. Placing food in the top, as shown in the small cage, saves money by reducing waste.*

rodent colony, let's make sure you understand what you're getting into. Unlike the fairly odorless and low maintenance characteristics of your snake, rodents are smelly creatures that can rarely be left for more than a day or two without being tended. What will you do if you go on vacation? Mice and rats generally keep themselves quite clean, but the odor of their urine is something that will soon permeate the entire building in which they are kept. A complete change of substrate, along with scrubbing the cage, is necessary on a weekly basis to adequately control odor. To choose the best location for your colony, you will have to consider temperature as well as odor dispersal. Rodents fare and breed best when maintained at a temperature of 70–80°F (21–27°C). At higher tempera-

tures, breeding activity decreases and urine output increases.

### Expenses

Besides start-up expenses, expenditures for food, substrate, and equipment replacement will be continuous. Food can consist of high-protein dry dog food, or the more expensive but nutritionally balanced laboratory rodent chow. Aspen shavings purchased in tightly packed bales make an economical substrate, but avoid cedar, pine, and other aromatic wood types. Always buy in bulk for savings. As for equipment, rodents are notorious for gnawing everything in sight, including water bottles. If the apparatus is to be placed inside the cage, glass bottles with metal supports and tubes will hold up better than plastic.

## Cages and Accessories for Rodents

Choosing cages and accessories for your rodent colony will depend on the number of rodents you wish to breed. If all you need is a few live mouse pinkies or rat pups, a single breeding group of one male and three to four females can be set up in a standard glass aquarium. The 10-gallon (38 L) size is appropriate for mice, and the 20-gallon (76 L) size can house the much larger rats. Having an extra aquarium available makes complete cage changes a snap. The clean cage can be prepared with pine shavings, and the water bottle and other cage accessories transferred, before moving the rodents themselves. When litters of pinkies must be moved, scoop the whole batch up with a paper cup or other makeshift scoop and deposit them in the same location of the new cage. Although rodents require nothing more than absorbent substrate, a water bottle, and food, they do enjoy and make regular use of hiding places, and will typically choose such secluded sites exclusively when giving birth. For a colony consisting of only a few breeding groups, I prefer to provide hard plastic hide boxes and perhaps a section of hard plastic tubing for a little variety. This would be an unnecessary burden in an extensive colony. Rodents are curious animals and excellent climbers, so a secure lid is as important for them as it is for your snakes.

## Trays

For breeding a large quantity of rodents, a rack system of sliding trays is generally used. Heavy-duty rubber or plastic trays such as those used in the restaurant industry for dirty dishes are ideal. Trays should have only rounded corners and edges inside, with no angles or depressions that can be chewed. Most breeders build

*Rack built for holding multiple trays of mice or rats.*

their own rack systems out of lumber and heavy wire. If you're not the do-it-yourself type when it comes to building things, check with local rodent suppliers to see if they have any new or used racks for sale.

## Litters

Female mice and rats produce average litters of 6 to 10 young each month, and may remain fertile for 8 to 12 months or longer. Breeding occurs again very soon after having a litter. They are social animals, and will often deposit their young together in communal nests. When disturbed, the entire group, including the male, may pick up pinkies in their mouths in an attempt to relocate them. Occasionally, the young may be eaten, especially when, through accident or oversight, food or water is not available. The young grow quickly, achieving independent "hopper" size within three to four weeks, at which stage they can be moved to a separate grow-out cage if needed.

*Health problems can be difficult for both boa and owner, but fortunately they don't have to happen. Follow a few basic guidelines to greatly reduce headaches and heartaches.*

## Prevention and Identification

The saddest part about many problems seen in captive snakes is that most could have been avoided. Let's recap several of the most critical points of boa care.

- Buy a healthy, captive-bred boa.
- Quarantine all new snakes.
- Provide a heat gradient, preferably from below, to allow a choice of temperature. Avoid in-cage hot rocks or lights that can cause burns.
- Increase humidity for tropical species, but never allow cages to remain constantly wet.
- Limit stress factors.

*An emerald tree boa.*

- Clean and disinfect cages and water dishes regularly. Replace water at least twice a week.
- Act immediately to correct any suspected problem before it gets out of hand.

Because of their whole-animal diet, nutritional problems are much less common in snakes than in other reptiles. The dangers of diseases and parasites, however, must be taken very seriously. It is too easy to avoid looking closely, to ignore or dismiss the signs, or to convince yourself that all is well, until the day the animal dies. Your boa deserves better.

Prevention of diseases and parasitic outbreaks begins by selecting only healthy-looking snakes. Problems are not always immediately apparent, so strict adherence to quarantine procedures is crucial. Having a fecal exam performed by your veterinarian will take much of

## TIP

**Sick Snakes**

Never buy a sick boa with the hope of doctoring it back to health.

the worry and guesswork out of dealing with new arrivals, and save you a lot of heartache later on.

The symptoms of diseases and parasites, especially internal parasites, are often similar. Basically, any unexplainable physical or behavioral manifestation should be a cause for concern. Symptoms to watch for include the following:

- refusal to feed
- regurgitation
- weight loss
- slow growth
- dehydration
- constipation
- runny, discolored, foul-smelling, or bloody stools
- lesions of the skin or mouth
- blisters or cysts
- swelling
- sneezing or wheezing
- inability or reluctance to close mouth
- lethargy
- neurological difficulties

If a problem is suspected, don't wait for the situation to get so bad that it is incurable. Place the animal in isolation and begin treatment immediately, or take the animal to a qualified veterinarian. Not all veterinarians are experienced in treating reptiles. I highly recommend finding one who is, and doing so long before his or her services are required.

Important knowledge can be gained even after death. It may seem unreasonable to spend money on a dead snake, but a necropsy (animal autopsy) can identify pathogens or lapses in husbandry that can improve the health and future care of your collection. Don't deny your mistakes—correct them! Deceased specimens should be refrigerated, not frozen, and delivered to your veterinarian as soon as possible.

# Treatment

Treating reptile diseases is a fairly recent and developing specialty within veterinary medicine, a field previously dedicated to the health of dogs, cats, and livestock. But before veterinarians began seeing enough cold-blooded patients to take much interest, dedicated herpetoculturists were already searching for cures for their reptiles' ills. Because of financial considerations, and perhaps the fact that reptile owners are often (but not always!) less emotionally attached to their pets than dog or cat owners, many herpetoculturists continue to treat their animals themselves. If you wish to pursue this area, entire volumes have been published on the subject.

The following sections are intended to familiarize you with some of the diseases that could affect your boa, emphasizing just how devastating those diseases can be, and how the efforts required to cure them far outweigh those needed to prevent them. Although some drug and dosage information is provided, it is not my intention to provide a step-by-step guide for treatment. I leave that to the experts, for the simple reason that not even the experts always agree. By reviewing the available literature and consulting with reptile veterinarians, I have determined that the drugs, dosages, and procedures that follow are generally accepted as being effective. In an area where recommendations are constantly changing, it would be inappropriate to say that they will be 100 percent effective, or that they represent the only course of action available. They are also not intended to be used for treating other types of reptiles, or even other snakes besides boas.

# The Danger of Parasite Loading

Many of the parasites that can harm your snake in large numbers are quite common in small numbers. Wild-caught specimens are often afflicted, yet seem perfectly healthy. So why should we worry? Because in the wild, internal and external parasite loads are naturally kept low through the processes of shedding and defecation, and the snake's habit of constantly moving on. External parasites leaving the host to lay their eggs are left behind to search for a new host. At the same time, thermoregulation allows the snake to always choose the best temperature for its defenses. Now consider your boa in captivity, where there is no escaping from feces or shed skins except through your intervention. The longer the snake is exposed, the better the chances for adult and larval parasites to reinfest the host. External parasites still leave the host to lay their eggs, but not only do they return to reinfest the host, but so do their thousands of offspring. The parasite loading continues to explode until the host's resistance completely fails.

# External Parasites

The two external parasites most commonly encountered on snakes are **mites** and **ticks**. Both are bloodsuckers, and as such can cause dehydration, anemia, and even death when present in large numbers. They can also be the cause of poor shedding and skin infections, and can act as vectors for spreading disease through your collection. Even in small numbers, they can be annoying to the host. An infested snake may spend hours or days curled up in the water dish, or cruise its enclosure endlessly, sometimes rubbing its head on walls and cage furniture. The result is a weakened, stressed snake that is now at risk for skin sores, as well as various infections from rubbing its mouth, nose, and eyes against possibly bacteria-laden objects.

## Mites

Mites can be difficult to spot, and even more difficult to eradicate once entrenched in a large collection. Your best offense is a good defense— never let them get into your collection to begin with! Mites most often arrive on newly purchased animals. Handling other people's snakes, or letting other keepers handle yours, is another way to pick them up, as is buying used cages or accessories and not properly cleaning and disinfecting them.

**To identify mites**, look closely around the eyes and in the fold of skin under a snake's chin. Mites are very tiny, and brown to black in color. They are more easily spotted when engorged with blood, at which time they may be nearly as big as the head of a pin. They are easily spotted on light-colored snakes such as an emerald tree boa or albino boa constrictor, but blend in well with the black markings and speckling of a common boa constrictor. The fine

*Mites, external parasites, can be found around the eyes and under the chin.*

white droppings mites leave behind can be a telltale sign on a dark snake. By holding these snakes up against a light background, you can search along the silhouette of the back for tiny, moving bumps. Wiping the snake with a white handkerchief, or soaking the snake in tepid (room temperature) water for 10 to 15 minutes should dislodge at least a few mites if they are present. A good magnifier is helpful in determining if a spot is a mite or just a speck of dirt. Dirt doesn't have legs.

**Mites are extremely mobile**, and leave the host to lay their eggs in corners, cracks, and crevices. If you discover that your snake has mites, assume they've spread to the cage and beyond, and immediately declare war. Simplify everything by having only a hide box, water dish, and newspaper in the cage. If small aquariums or plastic sweater boxes are used, swap the snake into a new one every day, with new paper, water dish, and hide box. Whether you decide to use an insecticide to kill the adult mites or not, the life cycle must be broken by destroying the eggs, which can hatch out within 30 hours of being laid. If the cage cannot be replaced daily, it must be washed and disinfected daily and the substrate replaced. Imagine that every crack and crevice contains mites and mite eggs.

**Treatments** to kill mites include the use of No-Pest Strips, Trichlorfon (Neguvon), Sevin Dust, and a number of commercial products such as Provent-a-Mite. Soaking the snake can also kill a lot of mites, but some will survive on the head and in air pockets under the scales. A 1-inch (25 mm) piece of No-Pest Strip, placed in an empty film canister with air holes punched out to avoid direct contact, can be placed inside or on top of the cage. Note of caution: Prolonged exposure to No-Pest Strips has been reported to cause nervous disorders in snakes, but this is still debated. Opinions on the proper length of exposure vary from two to three hours to two to three days, but certainly such strips should not be used constantly. Empty cages and accessories such as rocks and branches that are difficult to disinfect can be sealed up tightly with a larger piece of No-Pest Strip for several days, killing all mites and hatching eggs. Remove the strip and allow thorough airing before reintroducing any snakes. Trichlorfon, diluted to 0.16 percent (1/50 of normal product strength of 8 percent) solution, has been proven effective when sprayed on the snake and enclosure, allowed to air-dry and left for 24 hours. Sevin Dust (5 percent) can be liberally applied to the snake and its enclosure for three to four hours at a time. Always remove the water dish during any insecticide treatment and observe the snake closely for unusual breathing or behavior.

My preferred and proven method of treating mites is to use Mycodex flea and tick spray. The 0.2 percent pyrethrins spray is diluted with three parts water (to 0.05 percent), sprayed on a paper towel and wiped lightly onto the snake. The original cage is sprayed heavily, especially joints and corners, and after sitting for several minutes the excess is spread around and wiped out with a paper towel, leaving a thin film to air-dry. The outside of the cage and the shelves or rack on which it rests are also wiped with the spray, to help kill any egg-layers coming or going. If the snake must be placed back inside, the cage is first allowed to dry and air out for at least an hour. This process is repeated for two more days.

I prefer to transfer infested snakes to plastic sweater boxes in a separate room for a complete change of sweater box and accessories every day. I sometimes use the pyrethrin spray to treat the boxes before moving the snake in, but have generally found that wiping the snake down daily for two to three days, combined with daily box exchanges, quickly eradicates the mites. I then continue the daily box exchanges and inspections until I'm 100 percent convinced they're gone. The snake will also not be put back into its cage until that, too, is free of mites. If all snakes have been removed from the room where mites were found, I will even spray the carpet and behind shelves with common household bug spray, but I never use this type of bug spray inside or too close to my cages. Mites can survive weeks without a blood meal, so don't relax too soon.

## Ticks

Although much larger than mites, ticks are still often difficult to spot. Their dark, flat, rounded bodies can closely resemble the scales

under which they burrow. When engorged with blood, however, their size usually gives them away. Ticks are well-known carriers of disease, for snakes and humans. Snakes from a pet shop, especially known imports, should be checked closely. As with mites, ticks prefer protected areas such as around the eyes and the cloaca.

Once spotted, ticks should be pulled out with forceps or tweezers. Use firm, steady pressure instead of a sudden pull, so that the head is pulled out. A small amount of flesh, softened by the tick's secretions, may be pulled out as well, but this is fine. Treat the wound with hydrogen

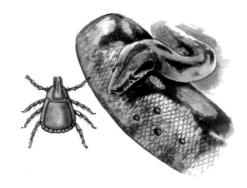

*Ticks are sometimes found on*
*newly imported snakes.*

peroxide or Betadine (povidone iodine), and finish up with Neosporin antiseptic ointment.

# Internal Parasites

Internal parasites can cause several different types of harm. At the very least, parasites living in the intestinal tract steal nutrients from the host. Heavy infestations can result in a healthy-looking boa that either loses weight or fails to grow, despite being an excellent feeder. Other parasites are not so subtle, sucking blood, boring through tissue and organs, blocking passageways, and spreading bacteria. In many cases, the existence of these parasites is not detected until necropsy.

Some breeders and importers dealing with large numbers of animals choose to treat all imports and new arrivals, using a range of drugs known to be effective against the most common parasites. If you have only one or a small number of snakes, a fecal examination by your veterinarian will give a much more accurate indication of just what treatment, if any, is required.

## Nematodes

Nematodes comprise a large group of worms, including roundworms, hookworms, and lungworms, most often found in the digestive tract but occasionally present in the lungs or airways. Roundworms present in large numbers within the intestine can steal much of the nutrients from the host, resulting in weight loss, malnutrition, or failure to grow adequately. Hookworms draw blood through the intestinal wall, causing inflammation, anemia, and peritonitis. Heavy infestations of lungworms can lead to pneumonia. Nematode larvae migrating through tissues and organs can cause direct damage or obstructions.

Although spaghettilike adult roundworms may occasionally be seen with the naked eye in stools or regurgitated food, detection of nematodes is typically made using microscopic fecal analysis.

**Treatment.** Panacur (fenbendazole), administered orally at a dose of 100mg/kg, is effective and extremely safe for treating nematodes. Repeat treatment every two weeks for a total of three doses. The ability of some nematodes to gain access to the host directly through the skin makes strict cage cleaning and immediate removal of feces imperative. Cleaning and disinfecting of water dishes, as well as close attention to personal hygiene, will help prevent the spread of nematodes to previously unaffected animals.

## Tapeworms (Cestodes) and Flukes (Trematodes)

Although unrelated, tapeworms and flukes are similar in their life cycles and methods of effective treatment. As adults, both can be seen with the naked eye—tapeworms as long, flat worms in the cloaca or feces, and flukes as short, dark worms in the mouth, esophagus, cloaca, or feces. Any parasites observed on the host can be gently removed with tweezers or a cotton swab. Kidney damage is also possible from renal flukes. Both groups have an indirect life cycle, requiring an intermediate invertebrate or mammalian host in which the larvae can develop. It is through the ingestion of the intermediate hosts that snakes acquire these parasites. The absence of intermediate hosts in captivity effectively prevents their spread through a collection. By using frozen food animals, further introduction is also unlikely. Despite their self-limiting nature, however, tapeworms and flukes are capable of causing internal damage and should be eliminated.

*Regular cleaning and disinfecting of water dishes and cages can help rid your boa of some parasites.*

**Treatment.** Droncit (praziquantel), administered subcutaneously or orally at a dose of 5–8 mg/kg, is effective.

## Protozoa

Protozoan parasites are naturally occurring and quite common in all reptiles. In the wild, most cause few problems, but under stressful or suboptimum conditions of captivity, the potential exists for these microorganisms to multiply to problematic levels. Diarrhea or foul-smelling stools, and stools containing noticeable blood, bile, or mucus, are typical indications. A fecal exam on a fresh stool can be used to identify the specific organism involved. If left untreated, some types, such as *Entamoeba invadens*, can spread to other organs and tissues via the circulatory system.

**Treatment.** The treatment of choice for boas is Flagyl (metronidazole), administered orally at a dose of 50 mg/kg daily for up to five days.

Another serious protozoan threat is the coccidian parasite *Cryptosporidium*, which has been responsible for some devastating epidemics in snake collections. As with many other internal parasites, these microorganisms can be spread through contaminated food and water, as well as improper hygiene. Lesions in the stomach caused by this parasite result in regurgitation of food. Swelling and thickening of the stomach wall follows, which can sometimes be felt externally or even seen. Cryptosporidiosis is an extremely contagious disease, for which early medical diagnosis is difficult and no cure exists. Any case of regurgitation for which no obvious explanation can be found, or where subsequent meals are also regurgitated, should be taken seriously. Isolation and diligent hygiene are a must. Euthanasia is often suggested for confirmed cases.

# Diseases

Snakes are susceptible to a number of diseases, both viral and bacterial. Although viruses have the potential to virtually wipe out an entire collection in a short period of time, it is bacterial infections that claim the most victims overall. Unlike the Gram-positive bacteria common to humans, the pathogenic organisms typically found in reptiles and implicated in many diseases and deaths are the Gram-negative bacteria, mostly *Pseudomonas*. Ross and Marzec, in *The Bacterial Diseases of Reptiles* (Institute for Herpetological Research, Santa Barbara, CA, 1984) report finding a 100 percent incidence of *Pseudomonas* in several boid collections examined, as well as in the water dishes of importers' holding facilities. Nearly every snake processed through the pet trade can be expected to harbor *Pseudomonas*, and possibly other Gram-negative bacteria, by the time it arrives in your collection. Because bacteria can be passed from snake to snake, and from female directly to offspring, even purchasing a captive-bred juvenile directly from the source will not guarantee a pathogen-free snake.

Bacteria are opportunistic, often benign in low concentrations but always waiting for an injury, stress, or weakness in the host to gain the upper hand. Providing your boa with the recommended warmth, while keeping it free of parasites and undue stress, will allow it to mount the necessary defenses to keep bacteria in check. Cages should be not only cleaned, but disinfected as well. Cleaning solutions are not always antibacterial, and disinfectants are not always good cleaning agents.

## Salmonella

Some bacteria occasionally found in snakes can be transmitted to people, perhaps the best known being *Salmonella*. Although rarely dangerous to healthy adults, there is an increased risk to very young children and those with compromised immune systems. Precautions include washing hands after handling snakes or cleaning cages, avoiding washing equipment and water dishes with the family's supper dishes, using antibacterial soaps and detergents, and limiting exposure of young children to animals and freshly shed skins.

## Inclusion Body Disease

Inclusion body disease (IBD) is an extremely serious retrovirus that affects boas and pythons. Whereas pythons often succumb quickly, some boas may carry the disease for more than a year before showing symptoms, meaning even a lengthy quarantine can't guarantee that a new boa is disease-free. The disease is untreatable, and the final outcome is death. Strict quarantine or euthanasia is a must.

*Stargazing or just looking up? When accompanied by muscle tremors or disorientation, this pose can be a sign of inclusion body disease, a very serious disease of boas and pythons.*

Symptoms of IBD may begin with regurgitation, progressing into head tremors, stargazing, disorientation, or paralysis. Stargazing, pointing the nose straight up into the air, can be a symptom of a number of possible diseases and conditions. Do not panic just because your boa is suddenly observed in this position. It may just be looking around, and freezing in any one position for several minutes is not uncommon. If the behavior continues, however, or is associated with other neurological problems, consult your veterinarian immediately for a diagnosis. Some causes may be treatable if caught early. For example, a nose-up posture is often associated with respiratory infections and other afflictions where mucus buildup makes breathing difficult. Wheezing or nasal discharge help identify such cases.

## Mouth Rot

Necrotizing or ulcerative stomatitis, commonly known as mouth rot, affects the gums and mucous membranes of the mouth. It is a serious, progressive disease that, if not treated quickly and aggressively, will spread into other tissues and bones of the head, resulting in death. Swelling and discoloration of the gums, in conjunction with an unwillingness or inability to close the mouth, are typical symptoms. Injuries to the mouth, such as rodent bites, abrasions from constantly rubbing the nose against screening or rough objects, and bruises from striking against glass can all lead to an increased risk of disease, especially when combined with a dirty cage or suboptimum temperatures.

**Treatment.** Treatment of mouth rot depends on the type and severity of the infection. In minor cases, infected tissues pull away very easily with little or no bleeding, leaving relatively healthy-looking tissue beneath. After cleaning the dead tissue away, rinse the area thoroughly with water and treat daily with Polysporin ointment. Neosporin can also be used, but contains less of the highly effective ingredient polymyxin B sulfate. In more serious and invasive cases, the infection goes much deeper. Affected tissues bleed easily and are not easily removed. Treatment requires injections of antibiotics such as amikacin, subcutaneously and possibly into the gums themselves. Effective treatment could take several weeks, even months. Removal of affected tissue, and possibly even bone, makes this a condition more suitable for treatment by a qualified veterinarian.

## Eye Infections

Although a snake's eyes are fairly well protected by the spectacles covering them, the fact that external parasites prefer to burrow around them plus the tendency of captive snakes to rub their heads along the glass surfaces of their enclosures make the eyes an entry point for bacteria. Symptoms to watch for include swelling in or around the eye, a cloudy appearance similar to preshedding yet apparent only in one eye, or the appearance of white or yellow pus under the spectacle. Immediate action by your veterinarian is required or the eye will be lost.

## Skin Problems

Inadequate humidity for tropical boas is a common cause of dry skin and poor shedding. Conversely, wet conditions or constant soaking may result in necrotizing dermatitis, also called belly rot or blister disease. Other wounds may be caused by rodent bites, burns, or noses rubbed raw on screen. Treat with Polysporin ointment and correct the underlying causes.

# CENTRAL AND SOUTH AMERICAN BOAS

*From dense rain forests to cool, arid mountains, the diverse habitats of Central and South America are home to the popular boa constrictors and rainbow boas, as well as slender tree boas and the massive anaconda. Isolated islands offer additional unique species and divergent populations of mainland forms.*

## Boa Constrictors— An Overview

The most popular boas by far are the true boa constrictors of the taxonomic species *Boa constrictor.* The taxonomy of boa constrictors poses many problems for taxonomists and serious collectors, and continues to be a subject of much debate. At the heart of the problem is determining not only which boas belong to which subspecies, but also whether some of those subspecies are even valid.

*Use plants and branches to enhance the display qualities of colorful arboreal species like this Amazon tree boa.*

### Subspecies

A number of subspecies are quite distinct in appearance and distribution so as to be generally accepted. On the mainland of South and Central America, these are the red-tail boa (*B. c. constrictor*), common boa (*B. c. imperator*), Argentine boa (*B. c. occidentalis*), and Bolivian boa, also known as the Amaral's or short-tailed boa (*B. c. amarali*). Some other named forms, including the Peruvian boa (*B. c. ortonii*), the Ecuadorian black-bellied boa (*B. c. melanogaster*), and the Peruvian black-tailed boa (*B. c. longicauda*), are considered by some to be undeserving of subspecific status, but merely color variations of the common boa.

### Island Boas

Several insular (island) forms of boa constrictors are also accepted as being correct,

*The colorful Hog Island boa may be extinct in the wild.*

based on their unique characteristics and isolation from other populations. These include the clouded boa (*B. c. nebulosus*) from the island of Dominica in the West Indies; the Saboga Island boa (*B. c. sabogae*) from Saboga, near Panama; and the St. Lucia boa (*B. c. orophias*) from St. Lucia. A small, light, and variably colored form of common boa known as the Hog Island boa, from Cayos Cochinos off the Caribbean coast of Honduras, possibly extinct in the wild, is being seen more frequently in collections.

## Most Common Boas

The two most common and popular forms of boa constrictors—the red-tails and the common boas—are also the source of the most confusion. Common boas, which are also referred to as Central American or Colombian boas, range from central Mexico through Central America and into northern and central South America. They are highly variable in pattern and coloration, and in habitat preference as well, rang-

ing from lush jungles to semiarid scrub and rocky hillsides. The vast majority of boa constrictors imported into this country in the past and today are common boas, most of which originate in Colombia. Most authorities agree that true red-tails originate only in the Amazon and Orinoco River basins of northern South America—eastern Peru, southern Colombia, Suriname, Guyana, and northern Brazil. Although red-tails are heavier bodied and can grow to a larger size than common boas, the differences can often be subtle. Particularly attractive specimens of common boa are quite capable of displaying the trademark bright red colors of true red-tails, and many imported specimens labeled as red-tails are in fact just brightly colored common boas. The pet trade in boas has served to confuse the issue further, creating additional common names based on color or locality.

Serious breeders have long recognized that even within a well-defined species or subspecies, incompatibility between specimens from widely separated locations is sometimes noted. The same can also be seen in specimens from different altitudes. The exact reasons are poorly understood, but may be related to incompatibility of reproductive organs or genes, or non-recognition of pheromones or courtship behaviors. In altitude-related incompatibility, the two snakes may have evolved to breed at entirely different times of the year, and may require different brumation strategies. Locality also gains importance when desirable colors or patterns are determined to be consistent within distinct populations. To meet the demand by breeders for more locality-specific animals, distributors began labeling red-tails with the country of origin, or in many cases, supposed

*Boa constrictors are highly variable in pattern and coloration, and in habitat preference.*

origin, such as Guyana red-tails or Suriname red-tails. Although ostensibly a good idea, several new problems arose. First, many common boas with bright red tails shipped out of Colombia began to be labeled Colombian red-tails. Second, red-tails for which locality data is missing are often labeled on the questionable basis of color or pattern alone. Lastly, it must be suspected that some red-tails, and common boas as well, are being collected in countries that ban their exportation and smuggled into other countries that allow exportation.

# Common Boa Constrictors

(*Boa constrictor imperator*)

So, what kind of boa constrictor is right for you? For most herpetoculturists, the common boa is the best choice. They are less expensive than red-tail boas, and yet superbly-colored and patterned specimens can be found with only a moderate amount of shopping around.

Both common boas and red-tails are excellent feeders on frozen-thawed rodents, and relatively simple to care for, so long as adequate space and temperature are provided. Both are typically docile, especially when captive-born and handled regularly. A possible exception is the northernmost population of common boas from Mexico, a dark-colored form often considered to have a less than pleasant disposition.

## Breeding

As previously mentioned, common boas do not grow to be quite as long or heavy as the red-tails do. Adults will range in size from 6 to 9 feet (1.8–2.7 m), and are also considered easier to breed. Like other boa constrictors, spur size is a good indication of sex, being very conspicuous on males. The gestation period is four to eight months. Particularly large individuals are capable of producing 50 or more offspring, although the average is likely closer to 20 or 30. Neonates may be susceptible to cold or dehydration, but under warm, humid conditions will often readily accept small mice soon after birth. As with any baby snakes, neonates may be a bit nippy, but they quickly calm down with regular handling.

# Red-tail Boa Constrictors

(*Boa constrictor constrictor*)

True red-tail boas set the standard by which all other boa constrictors are judged. Most are very light tan animals with sharp, bold saddles along the dorsum that expand in width and turn to vivid red bordered with black on the

*A very attractive Peruvian red-tail boa constrictor.*

anterior third of the snake. Heavier bodied than common boas, adult red-tails may grow to a massive 12 to 14 feet (3.7–4.3 m) in length, although 9 to 10 feet (2.7–3 m) is more typical. Gestation and litter size are similar to those indicated for common boas. Because of their larger size, and the consensus that they are more difficult to breed in captivity and that multiple males may be required to induce courtship, breeding red-tails may be better suited to more advanced herpetoculturists. Of course, if you desire a truly beautiful boa and have the means to afford and house it, don't let this dissuade you from purchasing a red-tail. Just remember that adults will eventually require a 6- to 8-foot (1.8–2.5 m) cage and feed on jumbo rats or even rabbits.

# Bolivian Boa Constrictors

(*Boa constrictor amarali*)

The Bolivian boa constrictor, also known as the Amaral's or short-tailed boa, is not as frequently available as other boa constrictors.

Bolivian boas occupy a range between the red-tail boas to the north and the Argentine boas to the south, occurring from eastern Bolivia and Paraguay, eastward through southern Brazil to the coast. Color is variable, but similar to common and red-tail boas, although in this subspecies the posterior red saddles are typically seen only on the tail. Maximum size is relatively short, only about 6 to 7 feet (1.8–2.1 m). The tail is also shorter than on other boa constrictors. Care is similar to that for common boas.

# Argentine Boa Constrictors

(*Boa constrictor occidentalis*)

The Argentine boa constrictor is an unmistakable dark boa, patterned in dark brown or black. It represents the southernmost race of boa constrictor, occurring in northern Argentina, southeastern Bolivia, and portions of Paraguay. It is listed as a CITES Appendix I species meaning special permits are required for both exportation and importation. Juveniles may display dorsal patches of pink or brown that typically also darken as the animal matures. Adults can grow to 7 to 9 feet (2.1–2.7 m). Argentines may readily exhibit the defensive posture of gaping the mouth at intruders and hissing very loudly. In my experience with a limited number of captive-bred specimens, this threatening behavior has been entirely bluff. However, to say that an Argentine boa's bark is worse than its bite would remain true only so long as there is no bite. If you can bring yourself to ignore the threat and handle the snake regularly, this behavior quickly disappears. Argentine boas are attractive animals, and with proper handling can become as docile as other more widely kept forms.

*Despite their reputation for bad temper, Argentine boa constrictors can become as docile as their more northern relatives.*

## Breeding

Due to their southern origins, this species may require somewhat cooler temperatures to induce breeding. They should not be subjected to constant cool temperatures that can result in serious respiratory infections. An eight-week period of cycling, using a nighttime low temperature of 60 to 65°F (15.6–18°C) and a daytime high in the low 80s°F (27–29°C), is a much better and safer approach. Argentines may not breed until after cooling has been suspended, rather than during cooling as with other boa constrictors. Gestation lasts approximately six months. Litter size may exceed 40.

# Insular Boa Constrictors

(*Boa c. nebulosus, B. c. sabogae, B. c. orophias*)

Insular forms of boa constrictors are less common in collections than their mainland relatives. Although generally smaller in size, they tend to exhibit darker coloration and subdued pattern. Some, like the clouded boa (*B. c. nebulosus*), are also known for having nasty dispositions. The relative scarcity of the insular forms serves to keep prices higher than for many other species. Herpetoculturists who keep them do so for the challenge involved or to expand their understanding of this fascinating and endangered group of snakes. With some island forms already thought to be extinct in the wild, including the Saboga Island boa (*B. c. sabogae*) and Hog Island boa (a unique population of *B. c. imperator*), the efforts of these breeders are to be commended.

# Rainbow Boas

(*Epicrates cenchria*)

As many as nine subspecies of rainbow boas have been identified, occurring throughout much of South America and on a handful of its coastal islands. Members of this species can grow to 5 to 7 feet (1.5–2.1 m) and are fairly similar in habits. All are patterned with a series of dark circles or large spots on the dorsum and sides, on a solid background in some shade of red or brown. The background coloration may fade at night, particularly on the sides, to nearly pure white. Their skin displays a high level of iridescence when exposed to the sun or other bright light, giving them their common name. A series of heat-sensitive pits can be found in the upper and lower labial scales, aiding the species in locating warm-blooded prey.

The majority of subspecies are rare in collections. The attractively colored Brazilian rainbow

*The iridescence that gives rainbow boas their name can be seen clearly in this Brazilian rainbow boa.*

*Less colorful than the Brazilians, Argentine rainbow boas are nevertheless intricately patterned.*

boa (*E. c. cenchria*) of Suriname, Guyana, southern Venezuela, and Brazil is by far the most commonly seen in collections. Exceptional specimens have a background color of dark orange to blood-red. The dorsal pattern is a single row of often perfectly circular black rings. A row of uniformly large, black spots, each containing a single, bright orange or yellow horizontal crescent near the top, adorns the sides. Smaller numbers of the drably colored Colombian rainbow boa (*E. c. maurus*), a northern form found as far north as Costa Rica, and an even smaller number of Argentine rainbow boas (*E. c. alvarezi*) are also kept and occasionally bred in captivity. The remaining forms include the Peruvian rainbow boa (*E. c. gaigei*), a beautiful form found in Peru and Bolivia that rivals the Brazilians in coloration, as well as *E. c. crassus* from Argentina, Brazil, and Paraguay, *E. c. barbouri* from Marajo Island off Brazil, and three additional forms all found in Brazil—*E. c. polylepsis*, *E. c. hygrophilus*, and *E. c. assisi*.

## Temperament and Care

With moderate interaction and handling, rainbow boas can become docile pets. They are extremely powerful constrictors, often wrapping tightly around the hands and arms when removed from their cages. A cage temperature of mid-80s°F (28–29°C) during the day and mid-70s°F (21–24°C) at night is ideal. Colombians may prefer slightly higher temperatures. High humidity is important, especially for Brazilians, and they should be observed for signs of dehydration. Regurgitation, poor skin condition, and difficulty in shedding are symptoms of low humidity. A large water dish or tub should be provided to help increase humidity levels and allow the snake to soak. Some specimens will be seen soaking regularly, whereas others may never soak, even when maintained under identical conditions. Rainbow boas have a high level of resistance to dermatitis, or blister disease (see page 51), and can be allowed to soak for long periods with less concern than would be appropriate for other species. However, for a snake that soaks day and night, try increasing the overall cage humidity by reducing cage ventilation and lightly misting the enclosure and inside of the hide box daily with water.

*Typical pale coloration of juvenile Brazilian rainbow boas. With adults ranging from an unpopular brown to the coveted bright orange "Lamar" phase, smart collectors will ask about the parents before buying.*

**Breeding** strategy for rainbow boas is similar to common boa constrictors, dropping nighttime temperatures into the low 70s°F (21–24°C), with associated daytime highs in the 80s°F (27–29°C). Argentines, being the more southerly race, may require slightly lower temperatures. The gestation period is four to eight months. Litters can number as high as 30, although Argentines produce fewer but larger offspring. All are excellent feeders on small mice. Neonate Brazilians and Colombians are born with lighter background coloration, assuming their adult shades of brown or red during their first year or two. This can make buying juveniles for future color-specific breeding projects a bit of a gamble.

## Insular Epicrates

In addition to the mainland *Epicrates cenchria*, nine additional species are found on islands throughout the Caribbean. Some species have been further divided into two or more subspecies, usually with home islands of their own. The small size of many of these islands, combined with growing pressures from human population, agriculture, tourism development, and introduced predators such as the mongoose have pushed some of these species to the brink of extinction. None of the insular *Epicrates* are particularly common in collections, which is unfortunate. Captive populations may soon be all that remains.

Four insular species of *Epicrates* grow to moderate sizes, with the largest being the Cuban boa (*E. angulifer*) at up to 12 feet (3.7 m). The others, capable of achieving lengths of 6 to 8 feet (1.8–2.5 m), are the Jamaican boa (*E. subflavus*), the Puerto Rican boa (*E. inornatus*), and the Haitian boa (*E. striatus*), of which eight subspecies can be found on several islands. As juveniles they tend to be arboreal, searching for lizards as prey, but they become more terrestrial as their size increases. The Jamaican and Puerto

*Eight subspecies of the Haitian boa can be found on several islands. This is the Cat Island Boa* (Epicrates striatus ailurus).

*The endangered Jamaican boa. Population growth and development for tourism has put many such island boas at risk.*

Rican forms are endangered, and listed as Appendix I animals by CITES. The Puerto Rican boa's specific name of *inornatus*, translated to "not ornate," might be said to apply to the group as a whole. Bright colors are not the norm, but whereas *inornatus* is indeed a dark snake with only a faintly discernible pattern, the others are attractive, shiny animals with dark, ragged crossbands on a light and occasionally bright background of red, yellow, gray, or brown.

The remaining species of *Epicrates* are even less commonly seen in collections. They are *E. chrysogaster, E. fordi, E. exsul, E. gracilis*, and *E. monensis*. The last form is also a CITES Appendix I animal. All are much smaller and more slender snakes, with body shape more closely resembling the rat snakes, and spend more time in trees and shrubs than do the larger forms. Coloration consists of dark spots, blotches, or crossbands, usually on a drab background of gray to brown. At least one species, *E. chryso-*

*gaster*, exists as both a blotched and a boldly striped phase.

Captive care for *Epicrates* is fairly uniform. Moderately warm temperatures and branches for climbing should be provided. Spacious enclosures have been suggested for the larger forms. No humidity requirements are noted, although high humidity may be helpful in eliciting courtship behavior.

## Breeding

Various species are reported to breed easily using nighttime temperature drops, misting with water, and using multiple males. Many, however, appear to be only biennial breeders. Litter size varies by species. Jamaican boas may produce up to 40 offspring, and Haitian and Puerto Rican boas as many as 25. All others typically produce a dozen or fewer. The young may prefer lizards, but may be fooled by scenting, rubbing a newborn mouse with a lizard.

# Emerald Tree Boas

*(Corallus caninus)*

Emerald tree boas are some of the most unique and fascinating animals of the reptile world. As the name implies, the overall adult color is a pale to sometimes stunning emerald green. Juveniles may be bright red, red orange, or brown, with small patches of green that spread over the entire body during their first year. The only pattern present may be a thin white stripe along the spine, and/or a series of thin, white bands or half bands, as if white paint had been dripped on the spine and trickled down. Labial and ventral scales are white or yellow. The large head is made even more pronounced by an extremely slender neck. Adults can exceed 6 feet (1.8 m) in length. Inhabiting lush rain forests of northern South America, the species is primarily arboreal, occasionally exploring the forest floor during nocturnal hunting. In the wild, they feed on a variety of small mammals, bats, and birds. Rows of extremely pronounced heat-sensitive pits in the upper and lower labial scales and exceptionally long, curved teeth give these snakes the ability to snatch hapless birds and bats right out of flight, although their nocturnal ways may mean that sleeping birds make up much of the diet. Juveniles feed on lizards and frogs as well.

Emeralds are perhaps best known for their trademark resting pose, tightly curled up on a horizontal tree branch or a Y-shaped fork, with the head resting comfortably in the middle. They achieve this pose by circling the body along the top of the branch in increasingly smaller circles until the body is tightly bunched. A strong but not excessively thick branch is usually chosen, so that, as the coils settle in front and back, they meet underneath the branch, providing a secure

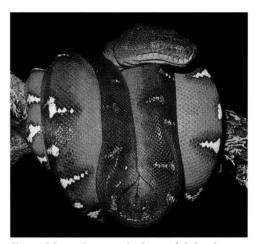

*Emerald tree boas make beautiful display animals, but are best left to experienced keepers.*

hold against wind or predators. Emerald tree boas often remain motionless in this position throughout the day, becoming active only after nightfall. If bothered in the resting pose, they may choose to bury their head in their coils rather than bite. The coils may also serve to collect rainwater for drinking.

## Amazon Basin Emeralds

Although no subspecies are currently identified, hobbyists generally recognize a separate phase, commonly referred to as Amazonian or Amazon Basin emeralds. These tend to be longer and heavier bodied, with a deep, dark green color, brilliant yellow labial and ventral scales, and a solid white stripe along the spine. Amazon Basin emeralds are also reported by some keepers to be quite docile. Maintaining either phase is best left to serious and experienced herpetoculturists. Although exceptionally beautiful display animals, emeralds can exhibit nasty dispositions and cannot be considered good pets. This is not to say that they can't become docile with regular handling, but this entails an almost daily struggle urging or prying them off their perch, with its inherent risk of getting bitten and of stress or injury to the snake. One look at an emerald's huge teeth is enough to convince most hobbyists that being bitten is going to hurt, and hurt a lot! Not long ago I purchased a pair of docile emeralds, but failed to handle them frequently. The female subsequently bit me on the back of the head during handling. I no longer keep emeralds.

## Care of Emeralds

If you're up to the challenge, emeralds require a large vertical cage with plenty of strong horizontal branches or perches. Provide a daytime temperature gradient by placing a spotlight or ceramic heat lamp over one end of the highest perch. High relative humidity is important, so include a large water dish or tub and control ventilation. Daily misting with water may be

*Juvenile emerald tree boas may be red, orange, brown, or green.*

required, especially during the shedding cycle. Some keepers mount additional water dishes to the side of tall enclosures near preferred basking spots, to help ensure adequate hydration. Emeralds are susceptible to respiratory illness and also a regurgitation syndrome, in which the animal consistently cannot hold down food. Refer to the section on regurgitation for information on causes and prevention.

**Meal size and frequency:** To avoid regurgitation and constipation in emeralds, it is imperative that feeding and defecation be carefully tracked and controlled. Feed young snakes every two to three weeks, withholding the next feeding if the snake has not defecated. Adults should be fed every three to four weeks, requiring at least one defecation for every two feedings. Only one prey item with a girth no larger than that of your snake should be offered, resulting in no more than a slight bulge after swallowing. If your snake has recently regurgitated, the prey should be no more than half the girth of the snake. Emeralds are sedentary creatures. Resist the urge to overfeed them!

Frozen-thawed rodents are readily accepted as prey, particularly when offered slightly warm. Feeding is best when attempted at night, after the snake has begun to wake up, and when food is offered from below using long forceps. Daytime attempts at feeding often result in the snake simply burying its head. Newly imported specimens may be difficult feeders, refusing to eat or preferring fowl or live prey. Males are reported to occasionally go off feed for several months. Reluctant feeders may be enticed to strike by leaving a live or stunned prey animal on the cage floor for the snake to observe and seize from above. Constriction and swallowing are accomplished while hanging from a perch.

*Cook's tree boa.*

## Breeding Emeralds

Breeding success for emerald tree boas is growing in frequency. This is encouraging news, as their unique requirements make the importation process tough on them. Captive-bred juveniles appear to exhibit far fewer difficulties than imports. Breeding is achieved as with other boas, by lowering nighttime temperatures to near 70°F (21°C), with associated daytime temperatures in the mid-80s°F (28–29°C) for a period of four to six weeks before placing the male and female together. Seasonal variation in humidity—high in summer and somewhat lower in winter—with heavy misting during passing low-pressure storm fronts, may help imitate the natural conditions and induce breeding. Copulation occurs arboreally, with the tails entwined and hanging below the pair. The gestation period is five to seven months, with 6 to 20 offspring being born in August to October. Neonates seem to prefer fuzzy mice as first foods. Many breeders maintain neonates in small glass jars or plastic boxes, with an inch of water on the bottom and a secure perch. The humidity and nightly swims serve the snakes well during their first year.

# Other Neotropical Tree Boas
(*Corallus*)

The other species of the genus *Corallus* are similar to the emerald tree boa in their arboreal habits and preferences, but generally more slender in build. These neotropical tree boas of Central and South America display amazing variety in both pattern and coloration, and several color phases may be produced within a single litter. They also rest curled up in trees, although not with the neatness of the emeralds. The eyes are quite large, aiding in nocturnal hunting.

The tree boas were subjected to several taxonomic reclassifications in the late 1990s. The Amazon tree boa, formerly classified as *Corallus enydris enydris,* was renamed *Corallus hortulanus.* The Cook's tree boa, formerly considered a subspecies, *Corallus enydris cookii,* was elevated to species status, *Corallus cookii.* Two other tree boas formerly considered part of the Cook's tree boa were also split off as unique species: the Central American tree boa, *Corallus ruschenbergerii,* and the Grenada Bank tree boa, *Corallus grenadensis.*

The Amazon tree boa (*C. hortulanus*) is perhaps the most varied in color and pattern, and by far the most common in collections. Adults average 4 to 5 feet (1.2–1.5 m) in length, but may exceed 6 feet (1.8 m). As their name implies, they range throughout the Amazon Basin and south along the coast of Brazil, in a wide range of habitat types. They are still imported in large numbers, keeping prices low, but imports often suffer from dehydration and parasites. Healthy captive-born specimens are increasing in availability as more keepers breed them.

All other species of tree boa are uncommon in collections and command high prices when available on the market. The Cook's tree boa (*C. cookii*) inhabits only the island of St. Vincent, and possibly a few neighboring islands, off the coast of Venezuela. It is a small snake, with adults rarely exceeding 4 feet (1.2 m). In the past, solid red and yellow Amazon tree boas were sometimes erroneously marketed as Cook's tree boas, but most specimens of this island form have a background of gray, brown, beige, or taupe.

The Grenada Bank tree boa (*C. grenadensis*) is found south of the Cook's tree boa on Granada and several islands of the Grenadines. Color and pattern variation in this form rivals that of the Amazon tree boa, with taupe and yellow being the most common background colors.

Central American tree boas (*C. ruschenbergerii*) range as far north as Costa Rica, southward into Colombia and Venezuela, and on the islands of Trinidad and Tobago. They are large, thick snakes,

capable of exceeding 6 feet (1.8 m), with a girth comparable to the emerald tree boa.

The annulated tree boas have also recently been reclassified. Previously considered three subspecies of *Corallus annulatus,* these secretive and poorly understood boas have been split into two distinct species. The northen annulated tree boa (*C. annulatus*) ranges from Guatemala southward along the Caribbean coast and in scattered locations in Colombia. The Ecuadorian annulated tree boa (*C. blombergi*) is found only in Ecuador. Color and pattern consists of dark, divided oblong rings laterally, sometimes meeting at the spine to form complete bands, on a background of red, dark orange, yellow, or brown. Adults average 4 to 5 feet (1.2–1.5 m).

**Care and breeding:** Although popular with a growing number of keepers for their varied colors, tree boas are noted for their unpleasant disposition. They are nervous animals, and the combination of prehensile tail and long, slender body allows for a long strike even when hanging from a branch. In other words, guard your face! They are not recommended for novice keepers.

For those who do keep them, however, tree boas are less susceptible to temperature, humidity, and regurgitation problems than the emerald tree boas. Most feed readily on prekilled rodents, and they make excellent display animals when housed in a tall enclosure with plenty of crisscrossed perches or forked branches. Adding live, hardy plants such as pothos not only provides a deep green background to highlight the snake's vibrant colors, but also adds cover and can help maintain the higher humidity required. Water dishes securely mounted at branch level are also recommended,

*Annulated boa.*

even though these snakes may spend a great deal of time on the ground.

Care and breeding are similar to that for emerald tree boas, although Amazon tree boas may be late spring breeders (Ross and Marzec, 1990). Offspring can number as many as 15. Neonates may initially require lizards or frogs as prey.

# Anacondas

(*Eunectes*)

Three species of anacondas, occasionally referred to as *water boas*, have been identified taxonomically. Only the green (*E. murinus*) and the yellow (*E. notaeus*) anacondas are generally seen in captivity. Inhabiting lush tropical rain forests of South America, the green anaconda is an olive green to grayish snake, with small black oval spots. Large specimens often measure 12 to 20 feet (3.7–6 m) in length, and are capable of exceeding 30 feet (9 m). Although the reticulated python may grow longer, the green anaconda's huge girth makes it the world's most massive snake. The yellow anaconda is much smaller in length and girth, growing to 10 to 12 feet (3–3.7 m) or more. The pattern of dark blotches is noticeably more dense than on its green relative, on a background of bright to pale yellow. It has a smaller range, occurring in southern areas of the Amazon Basin. The third species, the dark-spotted or Deschauense's anaconda (*E. deschauenseei*) from northeast Brazil, is not well known. All species spend a great deal of time submerged in swamps and sluggish rivers, providing them with protection, ease of movement, and concealment for ambushing

*Smaller than its green relative, yellow anacondas may still reach 12 feet (3.7 m).*

*The enormous size and bad temper of green anacondas makes them unsuitable as pets.*

prey. Birds, mammals, turtles, and even caimans (reptiles similar to alligators) are taken. Juveniles may include fish in the diet.

Because of their enormous size and tendency for bad temperament, only a limited number of yellow anacondas and even fewer green anacondas are kept in collections. Large enclosures with a suitable water pool are required. Copulation and even birth of the offspring typically take place in water. The number and size of neonates varies with the size of the female.

*The boldly striped rosy boas and the drably colored rubber boas represent the only two boas native to North America.*

## Rosy Boas
(*Charina trivirgata*)

Formerly known by the genus name *Licha-nura*, rosy boas have now been grouped into *Charina* with the only other North American boa species, the rubber boas. In an even stranger twist, the egg-laying Calabar boa (for-merly the Calabar burrowing python, *Calabaria reinhardtii*) of Africa was also merged into *Charina*. As with any such change, not every-body agrees, and the name *Lichanura* can be expected to appear on price lists for years to come. The rosy boas are a group of colorfully striped, diminutive snakes, rarely exceeding 2 to 3 feet (.6–.9 m) in length. In the wild they inhabit sandy and rocky desert areas of south-ern California, western and southern Arizona,

*Coastal rosy boas may be striped or unicolor.*

southward into Baja and northwestern Mexico. The species name, *trivirgata*, meaning "three stripes," is descriptive of the typical pattern, as most subspecies have three thick, evenly spaced stripes running the entire length of the body, on a background of slate gray, cream, or tan. Coastal rosy boas (*C. t. roseofusca*) of coastal northern Baja and extreme southern California are the exception, often having stripes so close to the background coloration that they produce a unicolor appearance. The dorsal stripe begins at the nose, and the lateral stripes begin at the eyes, which may be colored to match. Stripe colors vary by subspecies in thickness, evenness, and color, ranging from the orange or bright red of desert rosy boas (*C. t. gracia*) to chocolate brown or black in the Mexican rosy boa (*C. t. trivirgata*) of southern Baja, northwestern Mexico (Sonora), and south-central Arizona. Many herpetoculturists

*San Diego unicolor rosy boa.*

*Desert rosy boa. Small and docile, rosy boas are an excellent choice for a first snake.*

continue to recognize a fourth subspecies, the mid-Baja rosy boa (*C. t. myriolepis* or *C. t. saslowi*, depending on the authority), although it is not currently considered valid.

All rosy boas are similar in build. The tapered head is small and indistinctive from the neck, an adaptation common to burrowing snakes. The cylindrical body is short, yet stout, with an unusually soft or "squishy" feel. The tail is short and blunt. Subspecific determination is made based on locality, scale counts, coloration, and stripe characteristics.

In the wild, local populations of rosy boas may be quite variable in coloration, even within a subspecies. Small rocky outcroppings or canyons surrounded by open desert sands can serve to isolate a population as effectively as an ocean-locked island. As with many other variable species of snakes, a number of serious collectors and breeders have begun labeling rosy boas with locality-specific names, in order to preserve color, genetic, and behavioral traits that may have evolved within a particular population.

## Care and Feeding

Rosy boas are docile, low-maintenance captives, which, when combined with moderate prices, attractive coloration, and small size, makes them ideal pets. Some keepers report rosy boas delivering slow, deliberate bites, perhaps when gripped too tightly, although I have experienced this on only a couple of occasions. All are quite uniform in their captive requirements. They are active snakes that do a fair amount of climbing and yet do well in small cages. Low relative humidity and excellent ventilation are a

*Mid-Baja rosy boas typically have even orange stripes and are considered by some to be a unique subspecies.*

must. Include only a very small water dish of a type that is unlikely to be tipped over. Some keepers offer water only for a short period of time once or twice weekly, to reduce the humidity level and the possibility of spills. Rosy boas seem to prefer temperatures in the low 80s°F (27–29°C) and may take to the water dish when temperatures exceed 85°F (29°C). In my experience, regurgitation is common if daytime highs fail to reach 80°F (27°C). Wood shavings or sand can be used as substrate to satisfy their urge to burrow, but newspaper works equally well and is easier to keep clean. A snug hide box or hollow tube should also be provided.

As an adaptation to their harsh desert life, rosy boas seem especially adept at converting excess food into fat, and care should be exercised to prevent them from becoming obese. Small food items are preferred over large ones. Feeding one or two small mice once a week is sufficient, but cut back if the snake appears lumpy along the ventral or lateral surfaces.

## Breeding

Rosy boas are extremely easy to breed. Adults are springtime breeders, and can sometimes be bred after their second winter, although much better short- and long-term results are achieved by waiting until after the third winter. Best results occur after an 8- to 12-week period of cooling into the upper 50s°F

(13–15°C) or low 60s°F (15.7–18°C), although some breeders don't cool their animals at all. I have had success leaving them in a garage that fluctuated wildly during Florida's hot and cold spells from 54 to 78°F (12–25.7°C) from December through February, warming them back up in early March. Because rosy boas would naturally deal with cold weather by going underground, I do not use any additional lighting beyond the small amount finding its way around the garage door. After brumation, resume normal

*Gravid female Mexican rosy boa.*

been related to too-cool temperatures (dipping to 52°F [11°C] one night), failure to drink, or inadequate yolk/fat reserves (the neonates were three months old). One successful rosy boa breeder consulted for this book suggests it is often difficult to induce feeding in Mexican rosy boas, and that neonates are sometimes cooled into the low 60s°F (15.7–18°C) for a one-month "mini-brumation" immediately after their first shed. Other suggestions included changing substrates, using older pinkies instead of newborns, and even giving the neonates a rough ride in your car.

feeding for males and heavier feeding for females. Introduce pairs beginning in early April. Leaving them together, with occasional short separations, can improve the chance of successful copulation. Breeding typically occurs in April through June. A pronounced increase in girth leaves little doubt when the female is gravid. Females may cruise the cage incessantly if a warm basking site of 87 to 90°F (30.5–32°C) is not provided. The gestation period is four to six months. Small litters are the norm, usually numbering 4 to 10 offspring.

### Neonates

As with other boas, neonate rosy boas should be observed for signs of dehydration before their first shedding. Pinkies are often accepted as the first food. Some neonates may refuse food until their first spring. If all feeding tricks fail, some breeders suggest cooling the neonates as if for breeding and trying again after the spring warm-up. I tried this with three neonates, resulting in one death and one near-death within two weeks. The bad results may have

# Rubber Boas

(*Charina bottae* and *Charina umbratica*)

Rubber boas are the second type of boa found in the United States, occurring from southern California, east as far as Utah and Montana, and as far north as British Columbia, Canada. The southern subspecies (formerly *C. b. umbratica*) is now recognized as a unique species (*C. umbratica*). The form is patternless and quite shiny, being a nearly uniform shade of beige to dark brown or olive. Unlike most other boas, this species has large symmetrical plates instead of small scales on the top of the head. Adults seldom exceed 2 feet (.6 m) in length. These snakes spend much of their time burrowing in humid, loose soil or rotting logs in search of small rodents and amphibians. Birds

*The rubber boa is not a favorite snake because of its secretive nature and dull color.*

are occasionally taken. The tail is blunt and rounded, mimicking the head. A common defensive strategy is to gather the body into a tight ball with the head protected inside while offering the tail up to a potential predator.

Rubber boas are seldom kept by hobbyists because of their secretive nature and dull color. They prefer temperatures substantially cooler than other boas. Daytime highs in the 70s°F (21–26°C) and nighttime lows that drop into the 60s°F (15.7–20.6°C) or even 50s°F (10–15°C) seem to pose no problems. Wood shavings or mulch are acceptable substrates. The typical boa fare of small rodents make up the diet.

## Breeding

Much of the rubber boa's range receives freezing temperatures and snow during winter, making the species a spring breeder. Breeding them in captivity requires much cooler temperatures than for other boas, with nighttime lows approaching 55°F (12.8°C). Reduce or eliminate lighting during brumation. Breeding typically occurs in April or May, with offspring born in August and on into September. Small litters of three to eight are typical, and it is reported to be difficult to initiate feeding in neonates. Successful breeding may not be possible on an annual basis.

*Rubber boas are typically found in the western United States, stretching north to British Columbia, Canada.*

# OLD WORLD BOAS

*Old World boas include the wide-ranging sand boas, the unusual egg-laying Calabar boa, and three unique species from the island of Madagascar.*

## Overview

Boas are primarily New World snakes. However, a few Old World species do exist and have been growing in popularity in recent years. The sand boas of Asia and North Africa offer another colorful variety for those who prefer small snakes, whereas the boas of Madagascar can grow to several feet. The egg-laying and recently renamed Calabar boa of west-central Africa, formerly considered a python, is rarely kept.

Interest in the snakes of Madagascar, an island country off the southeast African coast, may have come in the nick of time, if not a bit too late. About 90 percent of Madagascar's animals, including a number of unique snakes

*The African sand boa.*

and lizards, and 80 percent of its plants are endemic, occurring nowhere else on earth. Unfortunately, the island is facing the typical problems associated with a burgeoning population. Deforestation caused by lumbering, slash-and-burn farming, and unrestricted cattle grazing has been devastating. Although the government has made serious efforts to protect some of its remaining critical habitats, it remains to be seen what the future holds. Madagascan boas are listed as Appendix I species by CITES (Convention on International Trade in Endangered Species of Wild Fauna and Flora). Madagascar currently prohibits their export, making continued propagation of the small number of specimens already in private collections problematic. Maintaining genetic diversity is difficult when most owners have no idea of the lineage of their boas. Responsible owners of these attractive Madagascar species should make every effort to avoid further inbreeding.

# Dumeril's Boas and Madagascar Ground Boas

(*Boa dumerili* and *Boa madagascariensis*)

Formerly assigned the genus name *Acrantophis,* the Dumeril's and Madagascar ground boas have now been merged into the genus *Boa* with the boa constrictors of Central and South America. Although the Madagascar ground boa is infrequently seen in collections, the Dumeril's boa is much more common. In the wild, the Dumeril's boa occupies the south and southwest portions of the island, and the ground boa inhabits the north and east. Similar in appearance, both species are relatively large, heavy-bodied ground-dwellers. A mottled pattern of browns, tans, and black provides excellent camouflage when lying in leaf litter. Particularly

*Slightly smaller but with all the positive attributes of boa constrictors, the Dumeril's boa is gaining in popularity.*

attractive specimens exhibit large amounts of pink or copper coloration.

Both species do very well in captivity following maintenance and breeding techniques similar to common boa constrictors. It should be noted, however, that Dumeril's boas come from dry, desertlike areas, and are therefore accustomed to drier conditions and less food than tropical boas. Both species will climb, but may feel more at home under a hide box or ledge, waiting to ambush their prey. Ground boas can grow to be 8 to 10 feet (2–3 m) in length, yet they produce relatively small numbers of large offspring, typically fewer than 10. Although smaller in length and girth, with an average adult size of only 6 to 7 feet (1.8–2.1 m), litter sizes for Dumeril's boas can exceed 20 neonates. Dumeril's boas are considered easier to breed. The gestation period for Dumeril's boas is approximately seven months, and eight to nine months for ground boas. A few specimens of Dumeril's have grown to nearly 9 feet (2.7 m). It has been suggested that there may be some intergradation where its range approaches or overlaps that of the ground boa, and that specimens from the northern part of its range grow larger. Overfeeding may also play a part. Whatever the reason, these giants are not common. If you would like a relatively large boa, yet are daunted by the thought of owning an 8- to 10-foot (2–3 m) snake, I highly recommend Dumeril's boas.

# Madagascar Tree Boas

(*Boa mandrita*)

The Madagascar tree boa, formerly known as *Sanzinia madagascariensis,* has also been merged into the genus *Boa* as *Boa mandrita.* An attractive boa, it still remains somewhat uncommon in collections. It may not be as arboreal as its common name implies, as specimens are often found in terrestrial locations. Adults can reach 6 to 7 feet (1.8–2.1 m) in length. Neonates may be born red, acquiring the adult coloration of green or grayish green during their first year. Some individuals from northern areas are yellowish, and an orange-brown "mandarin" phase is available. The skin is highly iridescent, with a bold pattern of irregular dark triangles traced with white or yellow alternating down the back, sometimes meeting to form hourglass-shaped bands. As with many other arboreal and semiarboreal boas, the Madagascar tree boa has conspicuous heat-sensitive pits among the labial scales. They are nocturnal hunters, feeding on birds, bats, and small mammals in the wild.

*Madagascar tree boas may not be as arboreal as their common name implies.*

Madagascar tree boas are reported to be fairly calm in captivity. Although some sources suggest captive care similar to that of the emerald tree boa, with vertical space and climbing opportunities, I know of at least one breeder who maintains the species in large blanket boxes on a rack system. Breeding may be achieved by placing snakes together and dropping the daytime and nighttime temperatures several degrees for a period of two months. Females grow noticeably darker when gravid, an adaptation that allows for increased heat absorption. Gestation is six to eight months, and the average litter size is 6 to 16. The young will usually accept very small mice.

# Sand Boas

(*Eryx* and *Gongylophis*)

Sand boas represent a growing group—11 or more species and several subspecies—of very

*Juvenile Madagascar tree boa.*

*East African sand boa. Yellow specimens like this one are often sold as Kenyan sand boas, and orange specimens as Egyptian sand boas.*

small, burrowing boas, inhabiting arid and rocky habitats from northern Africa east to Pakistan and India and north to Kazakhstan. Formerly all classified in the genus *Eryx,* three species are now separated as *Gongylophis.* Despite their wide dispersal, they are quite similar in appearance and habits. The eyes are placed high on a wedge-shaped head. The tail is very blunt, making it difficult for predators, and sometimes herpetoculturists, to tell at a glance which end is the head. The dorsal pattern typically consists of irregular dark brown or black blotches, or "splatters," in a single row along the spine or along both sides, sometimes forming an unbroken but jagged stripe. The background is pale to bright yellow, orange, tan, or gray. Pattern and coloration sometimes begins at the neck, leaving the head gray or beige and unpatterned except for a dark diagonal stripe through the eyes.

## Care

Adult sand boas rarely achieve 3 feet (.9 m) in length, with adult females growing significantly longer and heavier than adult males. Although sometimes ill-tempered, with adequate handling they can become quite docile, and their small size makes them suitable pets for almost any keeper. They are fossorial and

nocturnal in the wild, and in captivity will spend most of their time in hiding. A popular and natural choice for substrate is washed sand (avoid silica-based beach sand) to a depth of about 3 inches (7.6 cm), into which the snakes can burrow. Wood chips, aspen bedding, and newspaper are also suitable. A hide box is not necessary if the snake is able to burrow under the substrate. If newspaper is used, provide several layers for the snake to hide between, to keep it off the less sterile cage floor, as well as a small hide box. Good ventilation and a small water dish that is hard to spill are also necessary to keep humidity low. An under-tank heating pad at one end of the cage, or heating cable for a rack system, is recommended with a maximum surface temperature of 90°F (32°C).

Like other burrowing snakes, sand boas raid rodent nests in the wild, and in captivity may prefer pinky or fuzzy mice over larger prey. If frozen-thawed mice are offered but refused, try live mice. Sand boas often wait in ambush just below the surface for prey to walk by.

## Common Types

The most common types kept in captivity are the East African sand boa (*G. colubrinus*), rough-scaled sand boa (*G. conicus*), and smooth-scaled sand boa (*E. johnii*). Many breeders and dealers advertise pale East African sand boas as Egyptian sand boas and bright yellow or orange specimens as a subspecies, the Kenyan sand boa (*G. c. loveridgei*), although taxonomically this is incorrect. Other sand boa species include *E. jaculus, E. elegans, E. miliaris, E. somalicus, E. whitakeri,* and *E. tartaricus.* Two rarely seen forms, the Arabian sand boa (*E. jayakari*) and the West African or Saharan sand boa (*G. muelleri*), have even been discovered to lay eggs!

## Breeding

Sand boas have been successfully bred as early as 14 months of age, although most will first breed in their second or third spring. Successful breeding has been achieved without winter cooling, although some breeders prefer to cool their sand boas into the low to mid-60s°F (16–18°C) for a period of several weeks, and others drop the nighttime temperature to near 70°F (21°C) with a daytime high around 80°F (27°C) . These snakes often copulate while the female or even both snakes remain buried in the sand, with the tails protruding out of the sand at a 90-degree angle. Gestation averages from four to six months, and gravid females often take advantage of a basking site in excess of 95°F (35°C). The number of neonates varies by species, with maximum litter size typically being 12 to 30. Offering neonates several newborn mice at night will increase the likelihood of one being found and eaten. Some sand boas may not breed every year.

# Calabar Boas
(*Charina reinhardtii*)

The Calabar boa (*Charina reinhardtii*) of tropical west Africa is an unusual member of the boa family in that, like only two other sand boas, it lays eggs. Formerly known as the African or Calabar burrowing python (*Calabaria reinhardtii*), it has now been moved into the genus *Charina* with the rosy and rubber boas of North America.

The Calabar boa's similarities to the rubber boa are easy to see. They are short, cylindrical snakes, rarely reaching 3 feet (.9 m). Coloration is typically black, dark brown, or red, with groups of tan or yellow scales scattered in no particular pattern. The tail is thick and rounded, sometimes darker in color and offset by a white spot or band. When threatened, the snake often curls into a tight ball and presents the tail as a decoy head.

Although not commonly kept or bred, these snakes are very docile and appear relatively easy to care for. Provide a temperature gradient into the mid-80s°F (28–29°C), with wood shavings or several layers of newspaper for hiding. If burrowing is not possible, use multiple snug hide boxes in varying temperature zones. Calabar boas inhabit moist forests, not deserts, so water should always be available, and occasional misting may be helpful. Because they raid rodent nests in the wild, fuzzy mice and rats are often the preferred food.

**Breeding:** Breeding success has been rare. Females lay up to five large eggs for their size, often more than 70 grams each. The total clutch weight may be more than half the female's prelaying body weight, so it is imperative that she be sufficiently large and well fed to breed. The eggs can be incubated on slightly moist vermiculite at 82 to 88°F (28-31°C).

# PACIFIC BOAS

*At least four species of Pacific boas, also known as bevel-nosed boas, have been identified. With tens of thousands of islands in Indonesia and the South Pacific, more species are sure to be discovered.*

## Pacific Boas

*(Candoia)*

Four species of small to moderate-sized boas inhabit a number of South Pacific islands, including New Guinea, Fiji, and the Solomons. Where their home ranges overlap, the different habitat preferences of *Candoia* allow them to successfully coexist. All have keeled scales and a flat, angled rostral scale giving the appearance of a sharply pointed snout when viewed from the side. This feature has earned them their other common name, the bevel-nosed boas. Far removed geographically from other types of boas, the ancestors of these snakes likely arrived on current-driven rafts of vegetation from South America, a theory supported by the additional presence on Fiji of relatives of the green iguana.

*Pacific Island boa.*

The largest and most arboreal species of *Candoia* is the Fiji boa (*C. bibroni bibroni*), a slender, 5- to 6-foot (1.5–1.8 m) snake of the Fiji, Samoan, Solomon, New Hebrides, and Loyalty islands. One subspecies, the Solomon Islands tree boa (*C. b. australis*), is recognized. Occupying the middle ground is the semiarboreal Indonesian or Pacific ground boa (*C. carinata carinata*), a slender, 2- to 3-foot (.6–.9 m) snake occurring on New Guinea, the Solomons, and surrounding islands. One additional subspecies, the Solomon Islands ground boa (*C. c. paulsoni*), is recognized. The viper boa (*C. aspera*), a short, stocky mimic of the death adder (*Acanthophis*), is a ground-dweller, also of New Guinea, the Bismarck archipelago, and surrounding islands. Adults grow to just over 3 feet (.9 m). The fourth species, *C. superciliosa* of Palau, has only recently been recognized, and little is known of its habits. A number of additional *Candoia* subspecies have also been

*Coloration and pattern are highly variable in Pacific boas.*

proposed. With thousands of South Pacific islands, undoubtedly this group will see many changes in the future.

C. *bibroni* and C. *carinata* are highly variable in coloration and pattern. C. *bibroni* may be pale brown, gray, or red, heavily patterned with dark blotches and spots or even patternless. C. *carinata* are typically some shade of beige or brown, with either blotches or a wide continuous but ragged dorsal stripe. Colors may lighten at night. Viper boas exhibit wide brown or black bands on a background of yellow, tan, or reddish brown. The scales are heavily keeled. Viper boas may prefer higher humidity than the other Pacific boas.

## Care and Breeding

Pacific boas are now seen fairly regularly at reptile dealers and shows, particularly C. *carinata*. Captive maintenance and breeding requirements are similar to other boas, taking into account the degree of arboreal preference of the species being kept. Temperatures in the low 80s°F (27–28°C) are preferred, with a winter nighttime cooling to induce breeding. Neonates may be difficult to get started, preferring tiny geckos or other lizards or frogs, or parts thereof, for food, but can usually be switched to scented pinkies. Some specimens may prefer lizards exclusively, even as adults.

*Top and middle:
Two Pacific
ground boas.*

*Bottom: A Solomon
Island ground boa (left)
and a Solomon Island
tree boa (right).*

# BREEDING

*Captive breeding supplies modern herpetoculturists with the healthiest and most colorful boas on the market—and occasionally an unexpected surprise. Weigh the risks and rewards before breeding your boas.*

## Should You Breed Your Boas?

Breeding your boas can add an exciting element to your hobby. Even if your attempts fail, it is just as important to know what doesn't work as to know what does. By breeding your boas, you will be contributing your snakes' genes to future generations. Your offspring, whether sold to help pay for your hobby or traded for other species you may be interested in, can help reduce the demand on wild populations.

Breeding boas, however, is not without risks. Many breeders use a period of cooling called *brumation* to trigger the breeding cycle. Because such cooling does not occur naturally in the tropics, the experimental temperatures used have varied widely from breeder to

*Albino boas and other genetic color and pattern mutations can be very expensive.*

breeder. Unfortunately, the results have also varied widely. The bottom line is that some cooling may be beneficial for successful breeding, but too much and your boas' health will be at risk. Feeding must also be stopped during brumation, and this combination can leave boas weakened and more susceptible to disease.

With three egg-laying exceptions (two sand boas and the Calabar boa), boas are *ovoviviparous*—they bear live young. Because many snakes will not feed while gravid, the reproductive process can take a heavy toll on energy and bodily reserves. Considering the risks involved, only healthy snakes with good body weight should be selected for breeding.

## Age

Age, body weight, physical condition, and overall health are all key components to successful breeding. It is possible to feed some boas huge amounts of food, resulting in rapid growth, and breeding them in their second winter. This is often attempted by new breeders who think they see easy money coming. More than likely, however, the results include smaller litters and neonates, increased stillborn or deformed neonates and infertile "slugs," and a shortened life-span for the female.

Small boas such as rosy and sand boas can be bred after their third winter. This may also be possible for other boas as well, provided that they are at or near their adult size, with good body weight—heavy, but not obese. Males typically mature faster than females. If you can be patient and wait an extra year to breed a female, she will likely reward you with larger, healthier litters thereafter.

## What Is Brumation?

Unlike true hibernation, in which brain activity and bodily functions drop to near-zero, brumation is a period of reduced activity, in which

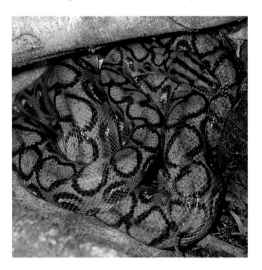

bodily functions are slowed but the animal may still move about. Brumation is more common in animals living in areas where winter temperatures do not remain below freezing. In the wild, brumating snakes will occasionally come out of their hiding places to drink, or to sun themselves on warm days.

The end of winter brumation signals breeding time for many animals, including snakes. The cool temperatures of winter are not just a timing trigger for behavioral patterns in snakes, but also appear to be crucial for physiological changes such as egg-follicle development in females and sperm production in males. Even for tropical snakes such as boa constrictors, which do not experience cold temperatures in the wild, a brumation period is considered helpful to achieve successful breeding in captivity.

Brumating snakes generally will not eat, and in captivity must not be offered food. Internal bacteria and parasites normally kept in check with warm temperatures may have the opportunity to overwhelm their host. For these reasons, your boas should not be exposed to brumation unless they are in perfect health, have been well fed before cooling, and have

*The end of brumation, a period of reduced activity, signals breeding time for boas.*

excellent body weight. Cages should be thoroughly cleaned, and clean drinking water should always be available.

**Note:** Some breeders avoid brumation completely, using only the shortening days of late summer and fall and a cessation of feeding to trigger breeding. Boas showing no interest are separated, the female is fed, and breeding is attempted again in three to four weeks. The secret to this strategy is to try, try again, and once courtship begins, not to remove the male too soon, as courtship may trigger egg-follicle development in the female.

# Initiating Brumation

If your boas are of adequate age, size, weight, and health, preparation for brumation can begin. Feeding should be increased for females during the months of August through October, especially for females having produced offspring during the summer. Just remember that the goal is a snake that is heavy but not obese. Fat snakes often have little interest in breeding. Feeding should be stopped in late October or early November, and the snakes given two weeks to completely digest and pass their last meal from the digestive tract. If defecation does not occur, try handling the snake or soaking it in lukewarm water. During this time, if you use cage lighting, adjust your timers to begin reducing the hours of daylight.

## Temperatures

Captive brumation for many snakes from North America and other temperate zones involves reducing the temperature into the mid- to upper-50s°F (13–15°C) and maintaining it at that level for approximately three months. The

*Juvenile common boa constrictor with its mother. All baby snakes can take care of themselves from the moment of birth.*

snakes are typically warmed back up in March, and breeding soon follows. Although this works well for rosy boas, exposing boa constrictors and other tropical boas to prolonged periods of constantly cool temperatures can result in severe and possibly fatal respiratory illness, and increased risk of other diseases. Therefore, a modified brumation is used for tropical boas, using only moderately cool nights but warm days. By slowly dropping the nighttime low temperature to approximately 70°F (21°C), and keeping or increasing the daytime high to 85–90°F (29–32°C), breeding can be induced while still maintaining a high level of resistance to disease. With the associated change in lighting, by the end of November, your tropical boas should be having long, cool nights, and short, warm days.

# Introduction and Mating

In mid- to late December, it is time to begin putting your males and females together. To avoid intimidation, the male should not be larger

*One of the male's two hemipenes is everted during copulation. Physical differences in hemipenis structure between species is one reason why crossbreeding snakes is rarely possible.*

than the female. One male can be used to breed two or even more females. Multiple males are sometimes used to elicit breeding, but of course the exact parentage of resulting offspring will be uncertain if the group is not observed. The enclosure used for breeding trials with multiple males should be sufficiently large, with multiple hide boxes, so that submissive males can separate themselves from dominant males.

It is possible to maintain a breeding pair or group together throughout the entire cooling period; however, a better breeding response is achieved when the snakes are kept apart and then introduced at the appropriate time. This

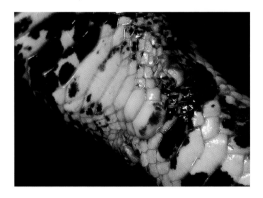

also reduces stress on the snakes, and because newly introduced snakes will often initiate courtship right away, the success of a pairing is less likely to be in question. Pairs or groups can be left together for days, or even weeks, occasionally separating and reintroducing the snakes if breeding activity is not observed.

## The Mating Act

Most breeders prefer to introduce the females into the male's cage. If the male is interested, he will immediately begin chasing the female, usually in quick, jerky movements, flicking out his tongue and rubbing his chin along her back. The male's spurs, located on either side of the cloaca, are sometimes brought into play to stimulate the female. A receptive female, typically moving slowly or with the same jerky movements as the male, will allow the male to rub his chin on her back as he aligns his body along hers, and may even lift her tail. When the tails are aligned, the male wraps his tail underneath the female, and inserts one hemipenis into her cloaca. Mating can last from a few minutes to a few hours. Occasionally, a female will lose interest before the male does, and may attempt to crawl away, dragging the male with her. Multiple successful copulations are recommended to ensure fertilization.

Most boa constrictors and other tropical boas will breed during the cooling period in December or January, and sometimes in February or beyond. Brumation should be terminated by gradually increasing cage temperatures to their normal levels beginning in late January. Resume feeding if the snakes will eat. If the female does

*The underside of a common boa showing spurs.*

*Female Brazilian rainbow boa with neonates and unfertilized slugs. Note wire mesh, offering neonates refuge from being crushed by the female.*

not show signs of being gravid, breeding trials should be continued through March. Argentine boa constrictors, coming as they do from more southern and cooler regions, can be cycled at a slightly cooler range of 60–65°F (16–18°C) for the nighttime low and 80–85°F (27–29°C) for the daytime high. Copulation in Argentine boas typically occurs after the end of cooling.

For rosy boas and other temperate-zone boas brumated at constant and much cooler temperatures, breeding also occurs after the arrival of spring. Terminate brumation at the end of February by slowly raising the temperature and hours of daylight over a period of several days back to the normal summertime schedule. After a few more days of warm temperatures, offer a small meal. Unless the meal is refused or regurgitated, resume normal feeding for the male and heavy feeding for the female. Begin placing the female with the male in late April. Rosy boas typically breed from late April through June. Continue separating and reintroducing the pair until several matings have taken place or the female appears to be gravid.

## Tips to Induce Breeding

A nonreceptive female will flee from the advances of the male, indicating that she is not yet ready to breed. If it is the male who is not interested, or if breeding attempts continually get no results, there are several things you may do to help. Introducing a male immediately after the female sheds her skin often gets good results. Don't even take the shed skin out of the cage.

Male combat may stimulate both sexes. Combat is often no more than a wrestling match to establish dominance and breeding rights, and typically no blood is drawn, but biting may result in severe injuries. Be prepared to remove the extra male immediately if biting is observed, if it is excessively fearful of the dominant male, or if the males constantly combat each other while ignoring the females completely. Even sexually immature males can be used in this role. The shed skin of another male may also be effective.

Other tricks to induce breeding include lightly misting the snakes with water and moving them into a new and unfamiliar enclosure. Passing storm fronts and low-pressure weather systems have also been credited with increased breeding activity. It is even suggested that placing the snakes together in a cloth bag and giving them a bumpy ride in your car might help.

# Indications of Fertility

Some breeders will take the opportunity immediately after mating to check on the fertility of the male. By inserting a swab into the female's cloaca, a semen sample can be obtained and transferred to a slide for observation under a microscope.

The earliest and best indication of fertility in the female is a midbody swelling as the mature ova are released from the ovaries. This swelling may be apparent only for a very short time, so it is important to examine females on a daily basis. Ova may be released before copulation and await fertilization in the oviduct, or even weeks after copulation and be fertilized by retained sperm. Placing the female with the male when swelling, particularly if copulation has not yet been observed, may increase your chances of successful breeding.

# Care of Gravid Females

A gravid female will appear quite large in girth in the posterior two-thirds of her body and will usually cease feeding. A warm basking area, up to 95°F (35°C), should be provided,

either using a basking light or heating pad. Failure to provide adequate heat does not always prolong the gestation period, but may result in aberrant colors or patterns and serious health and development problems for the offspring. Excessive temperatures can also be extremely detrimental, perhaps more so than inadequate temperatures, making a temperature gradient even more critical. A female faced with only two choices—too cold or too hot—will often choose too hot. Aberrant appearances caused by poor gestation temperatures are defects, not inheritable traits, so don't maintain gravid females under suboptimum conditions in the hope of creating marketable mutations.

Most females will spend all of their time curled up in the basking area. A peculiar behavior of gravid females is lying on their sides, sometimes to the point of being nearly upside-down. Whether this is an effort to expose the developing embryos to greater warmth, or just to be more comfortable, is known only to the mother-to-be. Females may be a bit testy at this time, and should not be held or moved if it can be avoided.

## Feeding

Although gravid females will often refuse food, small food items should be offered occasionally and may be accepted. Feeding too often or feeding prey that is too large can cause problems, as the developing embryos take up considerable space in the snake's narrow body. Whether the snake eats or not, clean water should always be available close by.

*Many boa constrictors, such as this Brazilian red-tail, often begin life as gray juveniles, changing to brown, pink, and red as they mature.*

## Gestation

The gestation period for boas averages from four to eight months. As the due date approaches, the female may become restless and move away from the basking area to a cooler spot. At this point, there is not much more to do but watch and wait, and begin planning on how you will house and feed the neonates when they arrive.

# When the Offspring Arrive

Unlike mammals, in ovoviviparous snakes the embryos do not develop attached to, and drawing nutrients from, the mother. Instead, the process could better be described as unshelled eggs being incubated inside the female. Each egg is surrounded by only a shell membrane, with a large amount of yolk from which the growing embryo will derive its nutrients.

**Delivery:** After parturition (birth), neonates should quickly break out of their membrane. Occasionally one may need assistance. Premature neonates born with the yolk not fully absorbed should be kept moist by misting and quiet while absorption is completed. Placing a small hide box over the snake will help discourage movement.

## Protecting Neonates

It is rare for a boa to eat her young, although unfertilized ova are frequently consumed. With the large size of some boas, however, the chance does exist for neonates to be crushed in the confined space of a cage or hide box. For this reason, as well as for easier observation and accurate record keeping, each neonate

*The popular albino boa.*

## TIP

### Keeping Records

Keeping accurate daily records of temperature and behavior throughout the breeding process will help you repeat successful practices.

should be moved into its own cage or plastic shoe box as soon as possible.

## Feeding

Neonates will shed their first skin within several days after birth. At that time, you can offer a first meal of a pinky or fuzzy mouse or rat. Try frozen-thawed first, and get your neonates started right. If they continually refuse, try leaving a live one in the cage overnight (remember, we're talking harmless baby rodents without teeth here). Neonates have adequate stored energy from their absorbed yolks, so resort to force-feeding only after two to three months for large species, and one to two months for small ones.

After giving birth, the female will be tired and weak. Let her rest, and offer her small

meals to begin with, especially if she has not eaten for several months. If she has lost a lot of weight, or if it is very late in the year, it might be best not to try breeding her again during the next breeding season.

Occasionally, a female may be unable to deliver unfertilized ova or dead neonates. If your boa has detectable lumps after parturition, consult with your veterinarian for advice and possibly X-rays. Surgery may be required to remove the object. Failure to do so could result in permanent sterility or death for the snake.

# Genetics: Breeding a Better Boa

In recent years, the popularity of unusual color and pattern mutations has increased dramatically. Initial offerings of new strains often come with a hefty price tag. Juvenile albino boa constrictors first appeared for around $10,000 each. Later morphs such as salmon, coral, and Arabesque continue to attract high prices. Such financially rewarding snakes are in extremely high demand by breeders. But where do these snakes come from originally, and how can desirable traits be continued or even improved?

## Traits and Genes

Physical traits are determined by the genetic code contained within every cell nucleus, on paired structures called *chromosomes*. One chromosome of each pair is received from the mother, while the other is received from the father. There exists a specific region, or *gene*, on each chromosome that controls each physical trait, such as eye color in humans, or skin color in snakes. The term *genotype* is used to refer to a gene pairing, while *phenotype* describes the resulting physical trait. Some of the common color phenotypes in snakes are albino, leucistic (white), piebald (areas of white and normal color/pattern), xanthic (yellow), amelanistic (without black) or anerythristic (without red).

If both genes agree on what the skin color will be, the animal is said to be *homozygous* for that trait. When the two genes are for different types, however, one gene often dominates the other and determines the outcome. Such animals are *heterozygous*, carrying a *dominant* gene for one phenotype and a *recessive* gene for another. Recessive traits, such as albinism, can only be expressed when a recessive gene is paired with a similar recessive gene. The table on the next page shows the results of the three possible combinations of normal and albino genes. Dominant genes are always shown using capital letters, recessive genes using lowercase. We will use "N" for the gene for normal color and "a" for the albino gene.

## Inheriting Traits

During a process called *meiosis*, single cells divide to produce two *gametes* (egg or sperm cells). Each gamete receives one half of each chromosome pair, and therefore one half of each gene pair. During fertilization, a male and female gamete unite to form a *zygote*. Each chromosome finds and pairs up with its matching chromosome from the other gamete. The genes, once again paired, immediately begin influencing the developing embryo.

Unless both parents are homozygous for a specific phenotype, the offspring become a game of chance. However, by knowing the genotype of prospective parents, and understanding which genes are dominant and which are recessive, breeders can use tables called *Punnett squares*

| Maternal Gene | Paternal Gene | Result |
| --- | --- | --- |
| N | N | Normal coloration, homozygous for normal color |
| N | a | Normal coloration, heterozygous for albinism |
| a | a | Albino, homozygous for albinism |

N = dominant gene for normal color, a = recessive gene for albinism

to forecast the outcome. In a Punnett square, the genes of one parent are assigned to the columns of the table, and the genes of the other parent are assigned to the rows. The intersections of columns and rows show each possible pairing after fertilization. Let's look at a Punnett square for two boas, one homozygous for normal color and one heterozygous for albinism.

|   | N | a |
| --- | --- | --- |
| N | NN | Na |
| N | NN | Na |

Parents: One homozygous for normal color (NN), one heterozygous for albinism (Na)

Offspring probabilities: 50 percent homozygous for normal color (NN), 50 percent heterozygous for albinism (Na)

While Punnett squares show all *possible* pairings of genes, they show only *statistical* probabilities of phenotype ratios. With millions of sperm and possibly dozens of egg cells meeting at random, this does not preclude the possibility of all offspring having the same phenotype.

New genetic terms used in boa color traits are *incomplete dominance* or *co-dominance*. Unlike simple recessive traits that require two genes for the trait to appear, these traits can be expressed from a single gene, often expressed even more strongly when both genes carry the trait. This latter homozygous form is typically referred as the *super* form, as in super sunglow boas. Because these traits are more readily expressed in first-generation offspring, and can often be combined with other such traits to produce entirely new forms, expect to see new boa morphs appearing faster than ever before.

*A boa constrictor baby.*

# INFORMATION

## Magazines

*Captive Breeding*
P.O. Box 87100
Canton, MI 48187

*Reptiles*
P.O. Box 6050
Mission Viejo, CA 92690-6050

*Reptilian Magazine*
22 Firs Close
Hazlemere
High Wycombe
Bucks HP15 7TF, England
Available in the United States from
Serpent's Tale Books
464 Second St.
Excelsior, MN 55331

## Professional Journals and Symposiums

The following are herpetological organizations of a more technical nature, dealing with topics of natural history, behavior, morphology, taxonomy, conservation, and other scientific research, but they include members from all areas of herpetology and herpetoculture.

Society for the Study of Amphibians and Reptiles (SSAR)
Publishes *Journal of Herpetology* and *Herpetological Review*
*www.ssarherps.org*

American Society of Ichthyologists and Herpetologists (ASIH)
Publishes *Copeia*
*www.asih.org*

The Herpetologists League
Publishes *Herpetologica*
*www.inhs.uiuc.edu/cbd/HL/HL.html*

International Herpetological Symposium (IHS)
Each year the IHS is held in a different location, hosted by a zoological, herpetological, or herpetocultural institution.
*www.kingsnake.com/ihs*

## Internet

A web search can be the fastest method to locate herpetological societies in your area, as well as breeders, reptile shows, products, and advice.

| | |
|---|---|
| *www.kingsnake.com* | A popular site with links to all things reptile-related |
| *www.reptilesmagazine.com* | Home page for the popular magazine, plus more online content |
| *www.cites.org* | Convention on International Trade in Endangered Species |
| *www.corallus.com* | Detailed information and photos of the tree boas |
| *www.boa-constrictors.com* | The boa constrictors as nature intended, in English and German |

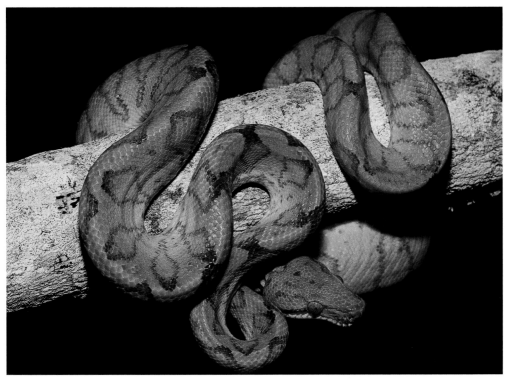

*Skin color and pattern are important factors when breeding and selling boas.*

## Books

*Rainbow Boas and Neotropical Tree Boas.* Hauppauge, New York: R. D. Bartlett. Barron's Educational Series, Inc., 2004.

*The General Care and Maintenance of Red-Tailed Boas.* Mission Viejo, California: Philippe de Vosjoli. Advanced Vivarium Systems, 1990.

*Neotropical Treeboas.* Melbourne, Florida: Robert W. Henderson. Krieger Publishing, 2002.

*Understanding Reptile Parasites.* Mission Viejo, California: Roger J. Klingenberg, DVM. Advanced Vivarium Systems, 1993.

*The Bacterial Diseases of Reptiles.* Stanford, California: Richard A. Ross. Institute for Herpetological Research, 1984.

*The Reproductive Husbandry of Pythons and Boas.* Stanford, California: Dr. Richard Ross and Gerald Marzec. Institute for Herpetological Research, 1990.

# I N D E X

## About the Author

Doug Wagner has kept and bred snakes for more than 20 years. He is a former president of the Suncoast Herpetological Society, based in Clearwater, Florida, and organizer of the annual Florida International Reptile Show, in Tampa.

## Photo Credits

R. D. Bartlett: pages 3, 5, 9 right, 17 top, 18, 23, 30, 32, 33, 35, 46, 53, 54, 56, 57, 60 left, 63, 65 top and bottom, 67, 68 top and bottom, 69 top, 71 top and bottom, 72, 73, 75 bottom, 81 top, middle, bottom right and left, 84, 89, 93; Zig Leszczynski: pages 4, 6, 11, 12, 13, 19, 22, 28, 42, 49, 52, 55, 58 top, 66, 70, 75 top, 78, 79, 80, 82, 83, 85, 86, 91; Bill Love, Glades Herp. Inc.: pages 9 left, 10, 26, 43, 59, 76, 87; Carl Switak: pages 17 bottom, 27, 36 top and bottom, 58 bottom, 60 right, 61, 62, 69 bottom, 74, 88; Mella Panzella: 39.

## Cover Photos

Front cover and inside back cover: Zig Leszczynski; Inside front cover and back cover: R. D. Bartlett.

## Important Note

The subject of this book is the keeping and care of nonpoisonous snakes. Snake keepers should realize, however, that even the bite of a snake regarded as nonpoisonous can have harmful consequences.

Handling giant serpents requires a lot of experience and a great sense of responsibility. Carelessness can be deadly! Inexperienced snake keepers and snake keepers who have small children are therefore urgently advised not to keep giant serpents.

Electrical appliances used in the care of snakes must carry a valid "UL approved" marking. Everyone using such equipment should be aware of the dangers involved with it. It is strongly recommended that you purchase a device that will instantly shut off the electrical current in the event of failure in the appliances or wiring. A circuit-protection device with a similar function has to be installed by a licensed electrician.

*All inquiries should be addressed to:*
Barron's Educational Series, Inc.
250 Wireless Boulevard
Hauppauge, NY 11788
**www.barronseduc.com**

ISBN-13: 978-0-7641-3404-3
ISBN-10: 0-7641-3404-3

*Library of Congress Catalog Card No. 2006042850*

**Library of Congress Cataloging-in-Publication Data**
Wagner, Doug.
   Boas : everything about selection, care, nutrition, health, breeding, and behavior / Doug Wagner ; with color photographs ; illustrations by David Wenzel.
      p. cm. — (A complete pet owner's manual)
   Includes index.
   ISBN-13: 978-0-7641-3404-3
   ISBN-10: 0-7641-3404-3
   1. Boa constrictors as pets. 2. Boidae. 3. Snakes as pets. I. Title. II. Series.

SF459.S5W34   2006
639.3'967–dc22                    *2006042850*

Printed in China
9 8 7 6 5 4 3 2 1